VOICINGS
FOR JAZZ KEYBOARD

by FRANK MANTOOTH

A comprehensive approach
to contemporary
keyboard voicings for the
PERFORMER
ARRANGER
TEACHER
JAZZ THEORIST

HAL•LEONARD®
CORPORATION

7777 W. BLUEMOUND RD. P.O. BOX 13819 MILWAUKEE, WI 53213

ABOUT THE AUTHOR

A pianist, composer, arranger, clinician, and educator, Frank Mantooth's five albums, *Suite Tooth*, *Persevere*, *Dangerous Precedent*, *Sophisticated Lady*, and *A Miracle* have garnered a total of eleven Grammy nominations in both writing and playing categories. Released on the Seabreeze label, the album, *A Miracle*, features Pete Christlieb, Kevin Mahogany, Diane Schuur, Pat LaBarbera, Bobby Shew, Kim Park, and other jazz artists.

As an author, Frank wrote five volumes of *The Best Chord Changes for the World's Greatest Standards* for Hal Leonard Corporation. This is in addition to over 170 works for combo and jazz ensemble which have been published with major publishing houses since 1978. Also recently published by Hal Leonard are a beginning improvisation method with accompanying play-along compact discs, two Christmas anthologies for solo piano, and the landmark treatise on chord construction, *Voicings for Jazz Keyboard* which has currently sold over 20,000 copies since its debut in 1987.

In February of 1999, Frank received the Florence Crittenton Foundation's Citizen of the Year award. Previous recipients have been former Kansas senator Nancy Kassenbaum-Baker and former First Lady, Barbara Bush. The Wichita Jazz Festival bestowed upon Frank the annual Homer Osborne award for outstanding contributions to jazz education. Recent notification has been received of Frank's inclusion in the third edition of *Grove's Dictionary of Jazz*.

TABLE OF CONTENTS

About the Author 2

Objective and Dedication 4

Acknowledgements 4

Foreword 5

Chapter 1. An Overview of Traditional Jazz Theory 6

Chapter 2. Generic Voicings (and the "Rule of Thumb") 8

Chapter 3. Generic Voicings Workout 13

Chapter 4. Miracle Voicings 15

Chapter 5. Workout with Generic and Miracle Voicings 17

Chapter 6. Voicing Suspended and Altered Dominant Chords
as Polychord Fractions 19

Chapter 7. Application of Polychord Fractions
in the ii7-V7-I Progression 25

Chapter 8. Voicings for the Blues and Other Common Progressions 31

Chapter 9. Voicings for Diminished and Half Diminished Chords 37

Chapter 10. Tritone Substitutions and Half Step Preparation 40

Chapter 11. The Melodic Soprano Voice (Melodic Comping) 43

Chapter 12. Sample Progression for Further Study 45

Chapter 13. Glossary 51

Chapter 14. Suggested Listening 52

Chapter 15. A Semester's Syllabus for a Jazz Keyboard Lab 54

Endorsements 62

ACKNOWLEDGEMENTS

I would like to offer a profound thanks to the following people who either influenced or helped with the compilation of this book:

> Tom Johns, who initiated the idea of this book; Eva Marie Heater and Mike Sweeney for editorial direction; Bill Harrison and Bill Sears for their help with the discography; Phil Feo for the professional job of copying the examples; and to Red, Bill, Wynton and all the great "compers" for their inspiration.

F.M.

OBJECTIVE AND DEDICATION

The majority of teachers in this relatively new arena of jazz education are not primarily keyboardists. This is no astute observation, just statistics. Most jazz educators have received advanced private instruction on their woodwind, brass, string or percussion instrument. Their educational experience with the piano was at best, functional (learn and forget the Star Spangled Banner); at worst, perfunctory (learn and forget all major and harmonic minor scales).

This book is dedicated to those of you with minimal keyboard experience. The material herein has been organized and verbalized in a manner that will result in better voicings overnight if the principles are assimilated and put into practice. And, obviously, if you can help yourself, you can help your students.

For those of you who can identify with any one of the following lamentations:

A. My keyboard experience is minimal so how can I help my pianist?

B. The published piano voicings seem so bland and uninspiring.

C. Publisher X puts out hip charts, but they use only chord symbols for the piano part.

D. My pianist has had x years of classical training . . . how can I help him/her with jazz voicings?

E. I can figure out the tertial textbook harmonies for chord changes, but is there any way to make these sound sophisticated?

F. My pianist plays all chords in root position and seems to be leaping all over the piano. Can you help?

THIS BOOK IS FOR YOU!

Enjoy,

F. Mantooth

FOREWORD

This is not a jazz theory book.

The subject of jazz theory has already been thoroughly examined, analyzed, and expounded upon by various redoubtable authorities, e.g. George Russell, David Baker, and Jerry Coker. This is, rather, a "how to" book. The book covers how to move between adjacent harmonies with minimal motion using good sounding state of the art voicings. The key words here are "good sounding".

Ex. A,1

The voicings offered in Ex. A,1 are, yes, theoretically correct, and the voice leading is smooth; however, Herbie Hancock or McCoy Tyner would probably not voice this progression in this manner. Although correct, they leave much to be desired in terms of sophistication.

Other texts offer various possible voicings for a given harmony.

Ex. A,2

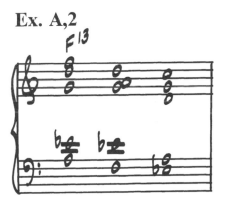

Ex. A.2 offers three credible voicings for an F13. However, these texts fall short by not explaining which voicing should be used in a particular progression. For example, the way one would voice a F13 in the progression C9 - F13 might be completely different from the F13 voicing used in the progression F13 - D+7($\sharp$9). The variable here is **context.** In other words, consideration must be given to 1, where you're coming from (i.e. the preceding harmony), and 2, where you're going to (i.e. the following harmony).

It is my honest aim to provide the aspiring pianist, arranger, or jazz scholar with a logical approach to the objective of smooth contextual voice leading with good sounding voicings. Regrettably, as with all worthwhile endeavors, study and practice will be necessary to achieve this objective. However, the material will be presented with the intent of easy systematic intellectual assimilation in hopes that undue drudgery can be avoided and that your involvement with music can be a fun and a rewarding experience.

Chapter 1: AN OVERVIEW OF TRADITIONAL JAZZ HARMONY

Jazz harmony, as all harmonic systems that we've come to designate as "Western," is based upon an equally tempered scale which uses the interval of a half step as its smallest unit. Albeit beyond the scope and intent of this book to chronicle the evolution of the Pythagorean scale to our currently used equally tempered scale, I'm still fascinated by the existence of other scales currently used in other civilizations. If we had been born three hundred years earlier, or if we had been raised today in an Eastern culture, say in China, this western notion of dividing an octave into twelve equal divisions would strike our ears as dissonant and unnatural.

The interval of the third is the basic building block of chord structures. Starting on an arbitrary tonic, we stack thirds (every other scale step) above the tonic to create the desired harmony. Incumbent upon the result of our third stacking is, of course, the parent scale or mode. In other words, different harmonies will be initiated depending upon the diatonic parameters of the scale or mode employed.

For example, let's pick an arbitrary tonic of "F" and construct a major scale.

Now, let's stack thirds and construct major family harmonies.

Since the 11th and 13th are dominant family constructions, the major ninth is the largest major family construction possible without chromatically altering the steps of the major scale.

From an "F", let's construct a Dorian mode, the parent scale for minor family harmonies.

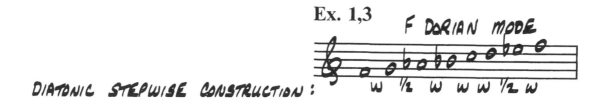

The resultant harmonies from stacking thirds within this diatonic system are:

Starting with an "F", let's construct a Mixolydian mode, the parent scale for all dominant family harmonies.

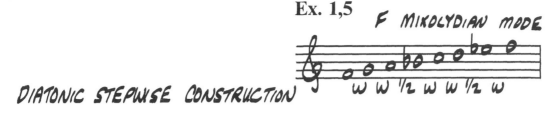

Ex. 1,5

When we stack thirds within this mode, the resultant harmonies are:

Ex. 1,6

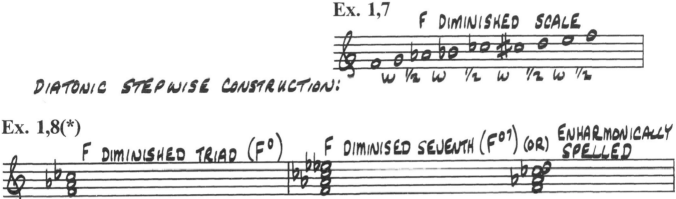

For diminished family chords, let's construct an F diminished scale and see the results of stacking thirds.

Ex. 1,7

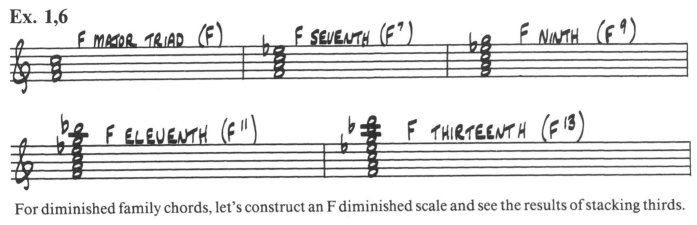

Ex. 1,8(*)

If we are to perceive augmented chords as alterations of major or dominant family constructions (depending on which diatonic system is used for the larger extensions), we have now covered four basic diatonic systems (i.e. Major, Dorian, Mixolydian and Diminished) which govern jazz harmonies.

One frequently heard and encountered exception (aren't there always exceptions) to tertially (see Glossary) constructed (stacked thirds) harmonies is the sixth chord.

Ex. 1,9   Ex. 1,10

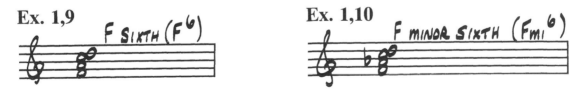

Our task is now to inspect alternative ways of voicing these harmonies. A favored means to contemporary sounding voicings is to "detertialize", or rearrange our stacked thirds so that the desired harmony is achieved, but the strict succession of thirds is avoided.

*When possible I've tried to adopt the chord constructions and respective designations as espoused by Carl Brandt and Clinton Roemer in their book, **"Standardized Chord Symbol Notation"**. However, with diminished chords, I must take issue with the claim that the $^{\circ}$ symbol indicates a 4-voice construction. Granted, in practice, the seventh step of the diminished scale may be played with no adverse tonal repercussions. But, how do we designate a simple diminished triad? The Brandt-Roemer solution of Minor triad with a flatted fifth, is, for my taste, too cumbersome. Therefore, I've elected to "stick to my guns", and refer to the $^{\circ}$ symbol as pertinent only to the triad. If a diminished seventh is desired, I'll use the symbol, $^{\circ}7$.

Chapter 2: GENERIC VOICINGS
(and the "Rule of Thumb")

Generic Voicings are five-note chord constructions which function for three basic chord families: major, minor, and dominant. They are simple to assimilate, easy to play, and avoid tertiality (see Glossary) while still accommodating the desired harmony.

The Rule of Thumb

Generally, with 5-voice chord constructions, the top three voices are played by the right hand, the lower two voices by the left. See Ex. 2,1.

In order to produce the strongest, most resonant sonorities, it's advisable to follow the "Rule of Thumb": Keep the right hand thumb in the octave between middle C and C1 (one octave higher). This rule helps players avoid muddy sonorities that can result when the right hand thumb moves below middle C.

Similarly, when the right hand thumb is above C1, the resulting sonority is generally too thin for comping.

Naturally, certain musical situations may specifically require a higher or lower sonority, but most frequently (particularly when comping), the optimal sonority will be obtained when the "Rule of Thumb" is intact.

Generic voicings relegate all major family chords into the category, "Generic Major". Major family chords include Major triads, Major Sixths, Major Sevenths, Major Ninths, and 6/9 chords.

Application: After determining that a chord does indeed belong to the major family, proceed as follows: First, place, the right hand fifth finger on the root of the chord and the second (or third) finger a perfect fourth lower. Then place the right hand thumb a perfect fourth lower. With the left hand, place the second finger a perfect fourth lower than the right hand thumb and the left hand fifth finger a perfect fourth below that. The result is a five-voice construction built entirely of perfect fourths.

As an example, let's say we see an FMa9 on a chart with no suggested voicing offered. The FMa9 obviously belongs to the major family, so we put our right hand fifth finger on the tonic and proceed as follows:

Due to the absence of the Major Seventh, the resulting chord is actually an F6/9. Theoretically, we do not have an exact FMa9; however, there are no offensive chord tones, tertiality has been avoided (in this case, restructured), and the right thumb is between middle C and C1. The chord is in the best position on the keyboard for sonority, and most important, the system works.

Generic Major voicings can also be constructed from the fifth scale tone of a given harmony descending in perfect fourths in a similar fashion as those constructed from the tonic down. For example, our FMa9 can be voiced in two ways:

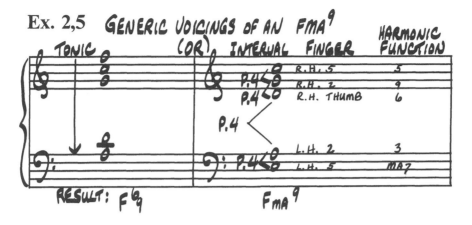

Ex. 2,5 GENERIC VOICINGS OF AN FMA⁹

With the generic construction descending from the fifth scale degree, we achieve an exact FMa9, but the point to be stressed is that either voicing is sufficient and context determines which we would use.

Let's observe the cyclical progression IMa - IVMa in the key of G: GMa7 - CMa7.

If we generically construct the G Major voicing from the tonic descending, and the C Major voicing from the fifth descending we derive the identical voicing.

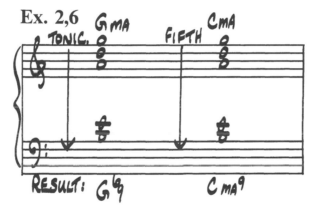

Ex. 2,6

Obviously these constructions would similarly function for any two major harmonies whose respective tonics are a fourth apart (e.g. EMa7 - AMa7, DbMa9 - GbMa9). Since the voicings are identical, voice leading has been minimized (in fact, eliminated), the "Rule of Thumb" has been observed for the sake of sonority, and the resultant voicings sound seemingly more sophisticated than the "third city" (see Glossary) rendition of the same progression.

Ex. 2,7 YE OLDE THIRD-CITY RENDITION OF G⁶⁄⁹ - CMA⁹

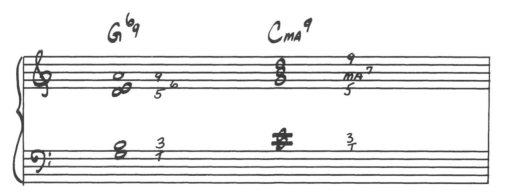

The generic minor voicing serves the following minor family harmonies: minor triads, minor sixth, minor seventh, minor ninth, minor eleventh, and minor thirteenth chords. To construct the generic minor voicing, place the right hand fifth finger on the minor third and, following the format for generic major voicings, use descending intervals of the perfect fourth to construct the five-note chord.

For an EMi9, we would start with the minor third and proceed as follows.

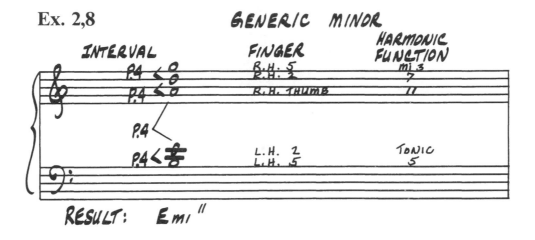

The chord produced is really an EMi11, a rough approximation of an EMi9, because the 9th is absent. Again, however, there are no offending chord tones, the "Rule of Thumb" is intact, and the resulting sound is tastier than the usual tertial (see Glossary) rendition of EMi9.

Let's now look at the progression, GMa7, EMi7, CMa7, or analyzed in terms of diatonic scale steps, IMa7, vi7, IVMa7. If we use generic voicings as follows, we can use the same 5-note construction for all three harmonies. The sound of each will be different as the bassist supplies the different tonics.

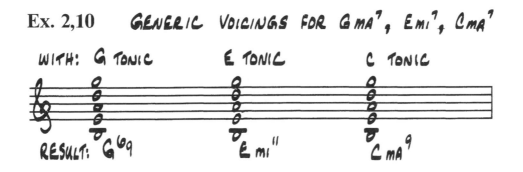

If we were playing the organ, we could sustain the same voicing and let the bassist "walk" across the different tonics. On piano, we would probably be obliged to play the same voicing with a rhythm stylistically appropriate to the nature of the tune, yet our goal of minimal motion between adjacent harmonies is achieved while at the same time avoiding "third city".

Generic Dominant Family Chords

Generic Dominant voicings function for sevenths, ninths, and thirteenth chords.

Building this category of chords requires a little more thought. The right hand begins as with generic major construction: Perfect fourths descending from the tonic or fifth of the given tonality. However, the left hand doesn't continue in fourths, but rather, plays the third and seventh of the dominant chord. The third and seventh are the most crucial tonal indicators of all the diatonic steps.

For example, to play a F9 (or seventh or thirteenth), place the right hand fifth finger on the tonic and proceed as follows:

Ex. 2,11

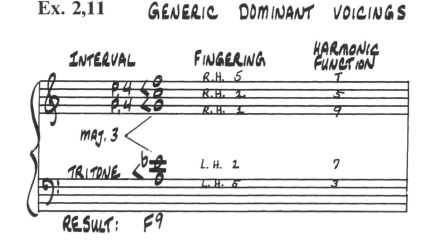

Similarly, the dominants, like the majors, can be constructed from the fifth descending.

Ex. 2, 12

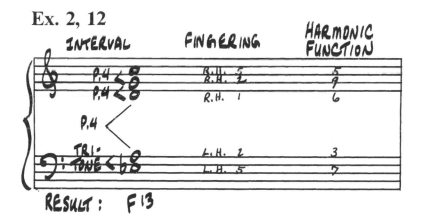

Note that the tritone between 3rd and 7th signals solely the dominant tonality. The interval between the third and the seventh of major and minor family chords is a perfect fifth.

Ex. 2,13

12   The tritone is reversed with the two different generic dominant constructions; when constructed from the tonic descending, the third is on the bottom. Conversely, when constructed from the fifth descending, the seventh is the lowest voice.

When we approach cyclical dominants, for example F7—B♭7 or I7—IV7, we can construct the F7 from the tonic descending and the B♭7 from the fifth descending to obtain minimal motion between the two voicings.

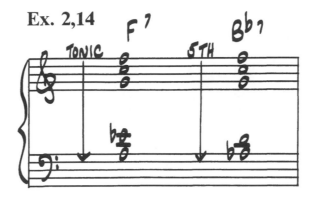

When voiced in this fashion, only the tritone indicators move while the right hand voices remain stationary. Again, tertiality has been avoided, the right thumb insures optimal sonority by observing the "Rule of Thumb," and minimal motion has been achieved between the adjacent harmonies.

Chapter 2 In A Nutshell:

Objectives:
1. Good sounding voicings that minimize voice leading between two harmonies.
2. "Detertialization" or restructuring of text book tertial harmonies.

Points to Remember
A. All Generic Voicings are 5-note constructions.
B. Generic Majors have two constructions. They may be constructed from either the tonic or the fifth descending in perfect fourths.
C. Generic Minors have one construction: all fourths descending from the minor third.
D. Generic Dominants have two constructions. They may be constructed from either the tonic down or the fifth down. The top three voices are quartal with the 3rd and Dominant seventh in the left hand.
E. Observe the "Rule of Thumb" (R.H. Thumb on the middle of the five tones played between middle C and C1). If context requires the R.H. thumb to dip below Middle C, be certain that the tonic replaces the lowest voice of the generic construction. This will be explained later in more detail.

Chapter 3: GENERIC VOICINGS WORKOUT

The most frequently employed progression in jazz and commercial music is the ii-V7-I progression. Let's use Generic Voicings to construct a ii-V7-I progression in B♭.

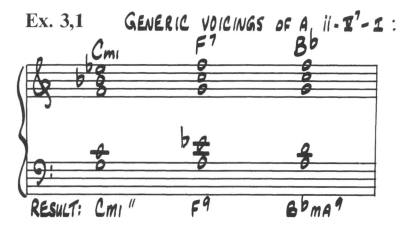

From the generic construction of C minor (from the minor third descending), I've moved as little as possible to the Generic voicing of the F7 from the tonic down. Resolution to the I chord, (B♭Ma9), is obviously easiest when B♭Ma9 is voiced from the 5th descending. We thereby have to move only one voice a half step.

Write and play the other sample voicings to acclimate yourself to the concepts of Generic Voicings and minimal motion between harmonies. Remember: move as little as possible and observe the "Rule of Thumb". Answers on following page.

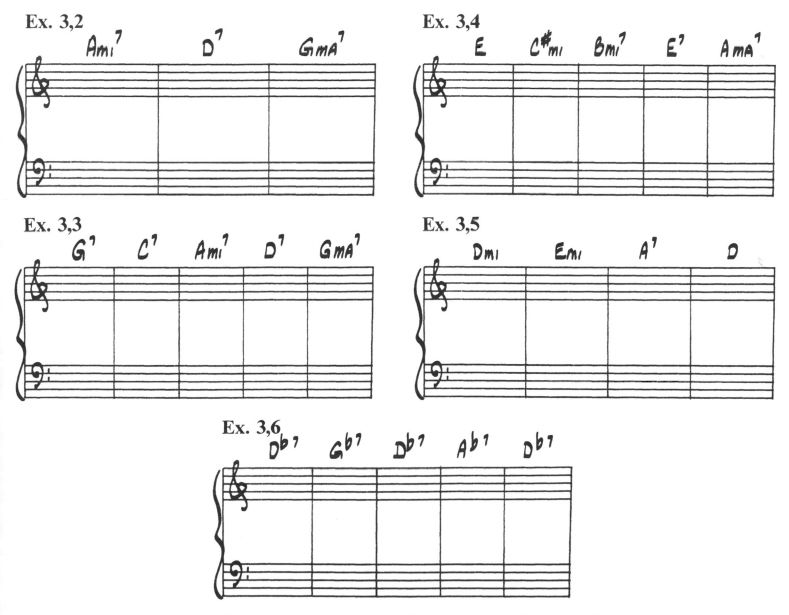

After these progressions have been played, practice Examples. 3,2—3,6 in all 12 keys.

ANSWERS

Ex. 3,2

Ex. 3,3

Ex. 3,4

Ex. 3,5

Ex. 3,6

Chapter 4: MIRACLE VOICINGS

You'll find the designation "Miracle Voicing" only in this book. The "miracle" aspect of these voicings is that they each accommodate five different harmonic functions (depending on which tone is used as the tonic), and they help us in our goal of avoiding tertial voicings. Like Generic Voicings, Miracle Voicings are five-note chord constructions.

Miracle Voicing I (M.V.I)

To construct M.V. I, start from any given tone (I've arbitrarily chosen an "E") and descend using the following intervals: Major third, P4th, P4th, P4th.

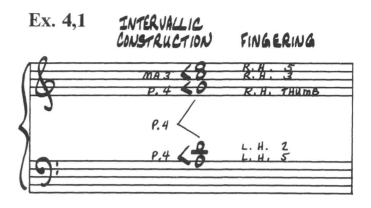

As mentioned, we can use this construction to accommodate five different harmonic functions:

Harmonic functions of Ex. 4,1. (M.V.I)	Tonic
Strong Major (3rd and 7th present)	F
Weak Major (7th not present)	C
Minor	A
Suspended Dominant (11th chord)	D
Lydian	B♭

To locate the tonic to be used for the various harmonic functions, use the following method:

1. The tonic of the strong major function, is ½ step above the top voice. In the case of Ex. 4,1: "F".

2. To find the tonic of the weak major function, use the second voice from the top of the construction as the tonic (root). In this case, "C".

3. The lowest voice in the construction serves as the tonic of the minor function. For Ex. 4,1; "A".

4. To find the tonic of the suspended dominant, or 11th chord function, use the second voice from the bottom.

5. The tonic of the Lydian function is either a tritone from the top voice, or ½ step above the bottom voice. In this case, "B♭".

In Lydian harmonies, the ♯4, or ♯11 is the most poignant tone as it is the only scale step which differentiates Major from Lydian.

Miracle Voicing II (M.V. II)

Miracle Voicing II is identical to our old friends, Generic Major and Minor. It is a 5-note construction, built entirely from perfect fourths. Like M.V.I, M.V.II serves five different harmonic functions: 2 Major, 1 Minor, 1 Suspended Dominant, and 1 Lydian.

Let's arbitrarily start from a "G" and descend in fourths as follows.

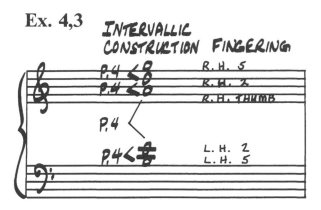

Ex. 4,3

Let's now find the tonics (roots) of the five different harmonic functions.

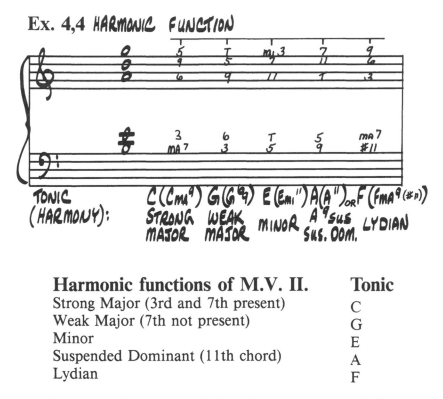

Ex. 4,4 HARMONIC FUNCTION

Harmonic functions of M.V. II.	Tonic
Strong Major (3rd and 7th present)	C
Weak Major (7th not present)	G
Minor	E
Suspended Dominant (11th chord)	A
Lydian	F

To locate the tonic of the 5 various harmonic functions, proceed as follows:

1. The top voice is the root of the weak major function. (Identical to Generic Major from the tonic descending). In this case "G".

2. Since the Generic Major voicing from the 5th descending is also identical to M.V. II, the tonic will be a P.4th above the top voice. In this example, "C". This is the strong major function since both the 3rd and 7th are present.

3. The 2nd voice from the bottom is the tonic of the minor function. In this case, "E". This construction is also identical to the Generic Minor with the minor third scale step as the top voice.

4. The middle voice is the tonic of the 11th chord or suspended dominant function. In this example, "A".

5. The root of the Lydian function is a tri-tone from the bottom voice. In this case, "F".

Note that for M.V. I the tonic of the Lydian function is a tritone from the top voice. Conversely, for M.V. II, the tonic of the Lydian function is a tritone from the bottom voice.

Chapter 4 in a Nutshell:
A. There are two miracle voicings designated as M.V. I and M.V. II. both are five-voice constructions.
B. Miracle Voicing I has a major third between the top two voices. Otherwise it is a quartal construction.
C. M.V. II is constructed entirely of perfect fourths.
D. Each Miracle Voicing serves five different harmonic functions depending on which tone is employed as the tonic.

Chapter 5: "WORKOUT" WITH GENERIC AND MIRACLE VOICINGS

Using only Generic Majors, Minors, Dominants, and M.V. I and M.V. II, let's voice some sample progressions bearing in mind the "Rule of Thumb" and minimal motion between adjacent harmonies. Remember that approximations of chord qualities (e.g. CMi11 for a desired CMi7) are permissible as long as there are no chord tones present which are not members of the parent scale/mode of the given harmony.

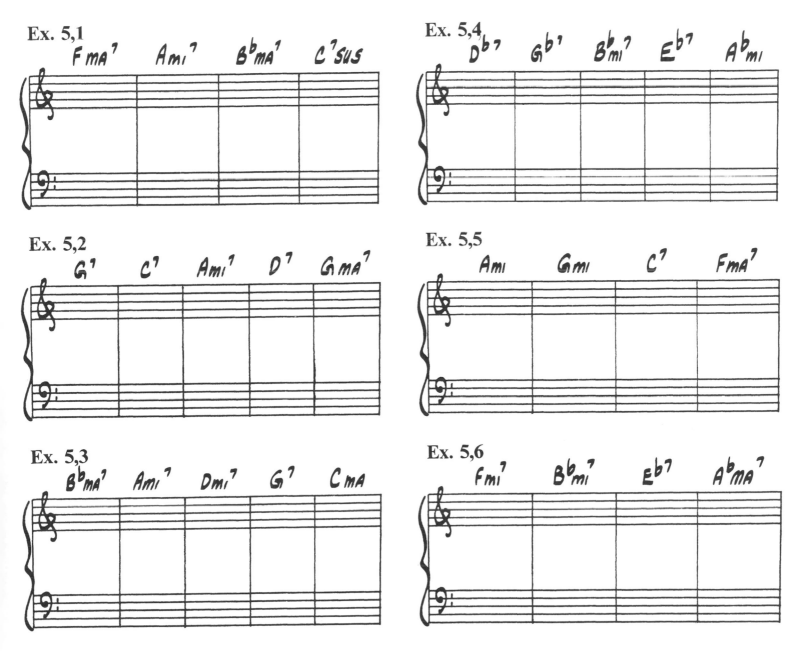

Answers on following page.

ANSWERS

Analyze the step-wise or intervallic motion of the root movements of each preceding progression and then transpose the progressions to other keys.

(∗) NOTE THE LEAP BETWEEN THE Dmi^{11} - G^{13} to OBSERVE THE RULE OF THUMB.

Chapter 6: VOICING SUSPENDED AND ALTERED DOMINANT CHORDS AS POLYCHORD FRACTIONS

Don't be intimidated by the title of this chapter. The concept here is as easy to assimilate as Generic and Miracle Voicings were in the previous chapters. Let's begin by redefining the terms used:

1. Dominant family chords: 7ths, 9ths, and 13ths. (11th chords are unique because in application the third is replaced by the 4th or 11th scale tone).

2. Alterations are diatonic scale tones which are chromatically raised or lowered (altered) to create new sounds or "tensions". Alterations to be covered: $\flat 5$, or $\sharp 11$, $\sharp 5$ or $\flat 13$, $\flat 9$, $\sharp 9$, and possible combinations of altered tones, for ex. ($\flat 9/\flat 5$).

3. To voice these altered dominants we're going to think of two harmonies stacked one on top of the other like a fraction:

$$\frac{\text{numerator}}{\text{denominator}} \quad = \quad \frac{\text{II}}{\text{I7}} \quad = \quad \frac{\text{G}}{\text{F7}}$$

General information and explanation of symbols used

1. "x" is any given tonality, e.g., F, B, E$\flat$, etc.

2. The Roman numerals in the fraction refer to the **major** scale steps of the "x" tonality.

3. Tritone indicators for dominant family chords are Ma 3rd and dominant seventh (the interval between these two tones is a tritone) with the exception of 11th chords (suspended dominant chords) where the third is absent. The Ma3rd and dominant 7th are the only mandatory chord tones for the denominator, or bottom half of the polychord fraction.

4. The "numerator" triad on top is always a major triad, and any inversion, i.e. root position, first inversion, or second inversion is equally functional as the "numerator" or top half of the polychord fraction.

5. Only in rare instances may we not take the liberty to consider 7th, 9ths, and 13ths as interchangeable. In other words, when we see a chord symbol designation of a 7th, the ninth or sixth (13th) may be added in performance thereby enhancing, not detracting, from the chord quality.

Let's start with the one exception, the 11th chord (or suspended dominant).

Desired harmony	Fraction	Example	Implementation
I. x11 or x7sus	$\frac{\flat\text{VII}}{\text{I}}$	C11	$\frac{\text{B}\flat}{\text{C}}$

This harmony is the one exception for two reasons:

1. It is not an altered harmony. All chord tones are in the Mixolydian diatonic system.

2. The third is not used in application, hence the tritone indicators for the denominator are not applicable.

However, conceptualizing the 11th chord as $\frac{\flat \text{VII}}{\text{I}}$ instantly gives us the best voicing. In the case of C11, because the third is deleted and the seventh is already present in the numerator triad, the obvious choices for the two representative tones of denominator are the tonic and fifth.

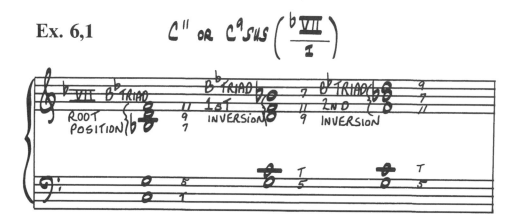

Ex. 6,1 C^{11} or $C^{9}sus \left(\frac{\flat \text{VII}}{\text{I}} \right)$

Note in Ex. VI.1. that all inversions of the major triad based on the $\flat$VII scale step (B$\flat$) are equally functional. In order to keep all voices as compact as possible, it is sometimes necessary to reverse the tonic and fifth in the left hand. Note that in the 1st and 2nd inversion spellings of Ex. 6,1, the tonic is now above the fifth in the left hand. Wide intervallic "gaps" between the two hands should be avoided in the interest of sonority.

Example 6,2 lists the polychord fractions to be used for other altered dominant chords.

Ex. 6,2   POLYCHORD FRACTIONS FOR ALTERED DOMINANTS:

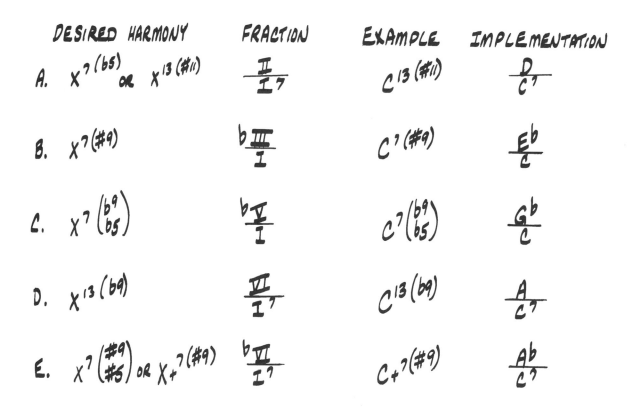

DESIRED HARMONY	FRACTION	EXAMPLE	IMPLEMENTATION
A. $X^{7(\flat5)}$ or $X^{13(\sharp11)}$	$\frac{\text{II}}{\text{I}^7}$	$C^{13(\sharp11)}$	$\frac{D}{C^7}$
B. $X^{7(\sharp9)}$	$\frac{\flat\text{III}}{\text{I}}$	$C^{7(\sharp9)}$	$\frac{E\flat}{C}$
C. $X^{7\left(\substack{\flat9 \\ \flat5}\right)}$	$\frac{\flat\text{V}}{\text{I}}$	$C^{7\left(\substack{\flat9 \\ \flat5}\right)}$	$\frac{G\flat}{C}$
D. $X^{13(\flat9)}$	$\frac{\text{VI}}{\text{I}^7}$	$C^{13(\flat9)}$	$\frac{A}{C^7}$
E. $X^{7\left(\substack{\sharp9 \\ \sharp5}\right)}$ or $X_{+}^{7(\sharp9)}$	$\frac{\flat\text{VI}}{\text{I}^7}$	$C_{+}^{7(\sharp9)}$	$\frac{A\flat}{C^7}$

"C" has arbitrarily chosen as the x tonality since most of us first learned the C scale and therefore feel at home in "C".

Let's voice the preceding:

Ex. 6,3

1. Note in the examples 6,3a-e, all possible inversions of the numerator (R.H.) triad are useable.

2. In examples 6,3b and c, the denominator triad does not include the 7th designation since the 7th scale tone is already present in the numerator triad.

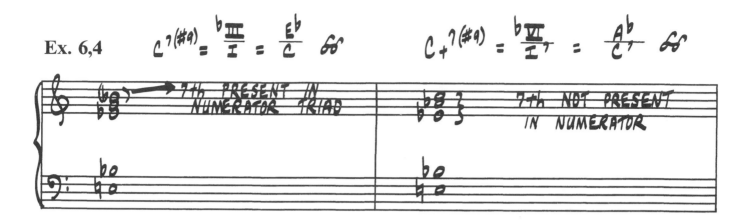

3. In all examples the denominator (L.H.) triad is represented by the two strongest tonal indicators, the third and the dominant seventh. When the third and seventh are already present in the numerator triad, we may substitute the tonic for the doubled note in the Left Hand.

Let's now attempt to voice random altered dominant chords and 11th chords as polychord fractions bearing three factors in mind:

1. The "Rule of Thumb".

2. Minimal motion between adjacent harmonies.

3. The right hand plays the numerator triad, the left hand plays the denominator.

Random altered dominants and suspended dominant chords.

F11, E♭+7(#9), G7(♭9/♭5), D7(#9), A♭13(#11), C7(♭9/♭5), F#9sus, F7(♭5),
D♭7(#9), E13(♭9), A11, B♭13(#11).

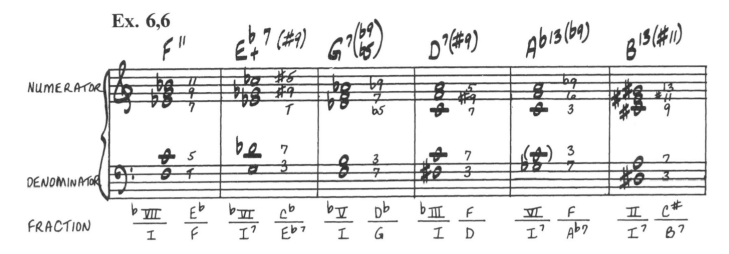

For the D♭7(#9) above, I've used E Major triad for the ♭III numerator triad rather than the theoretically correct F♭ Major to avoid double flats.

Notice the minimal movement between the numerator triads. For example, in the first harmony, F11, the root position E♭ triad moves to the C♭ Major triad in the first inversion by simply moving the top two tones a ½ step in opposite directions. The "E♭" is common to both harmonies.

Ex. 6,7

Motion between the D7 (#9) and the A♭13(♭9) is negated as both D and A♭ use enharmonically the identical tritone indicators for the numerator; ♭III Major triad in D, and VI Major triad in A♭ are both F Major triad, so there's no need whatsoever to revoice or move the tones of the numerator triad.

Two Answers:

1. By using this method of voicing, we instantly have a guaranteed state of the art sounding 5-note construction for the desired harmony.
2. Expendable chord tones are hereby deleted.

Memorize the 6 polychord fractions and review them until the association between the fraction and the desired harmony are automatic. For example, the (#11) alteration should ultimately trigger a mental response of $\frac{II}{I7}$.

In recapitulation, remember:

1. Suspended dominant chords are not altered dominants; however, the polychord fraction concept of $\frac{bVII}{I}$ not only works, but offers a palatable solution. Root and fifth serve for the L.H. denominator.
2. Tritone indicators (3rd and 7th) may function for all altered dominants as the representative tones for the left hand (denominator). However, should the third or seventh be present in the numerator triad, the tonic may replace the doubled tone in the left hand (denominator).

Paying heed to the "Rule of Thumb" and the concept of "minimal motion", voice the following progressions. Because root position, first inversion, and second inversion triads could feasibly place the right hand thumb within the confines of middle C to C1, only one answer will be offered. If you've moved as little as possible and adhered to the "Rule of Thumb", your voicings are equally correct.

Random suspended and altered dominants.

6,8a. A7(#9), C7+(#9), B13(b9), E9sus, D7(b9/b5), Db9(#11), F11, Bb13(#11), Ab7(b9/b5)
6,8b. D13(#11), G7(b9), C+ 7(#9), F7(#9), Bb9sus, A7(b9/b5), Eb7(b5), Db7(# 9), E7(b9/b5)

When the "Rule of Thumb" has been broken by placing the R.H. thumb lower than Middle C, or when a R.H. tone is doubled in the left, it's advisable to substitute the tonic for the lowest voice. The last measure of 6,8b demonstrates this principle.

Chapter 7: APPLICATION OF POLYCHORD FRACTIONS IN THE ii7-V7-I PROGRESSION

With the addition of Polychord Fractions as altered/suspended Dominants to our harmonic vocabulary, we are now capable of voicing familiar progressions with some degree of sophistication.

With voicings we've learned in this book, let's now play II-V-I's using various alterations for the dominant V7.

As before, the voicings will be 5-note constructions, which adhere to the "Rule of Thumb" and the principle of minimal motion.

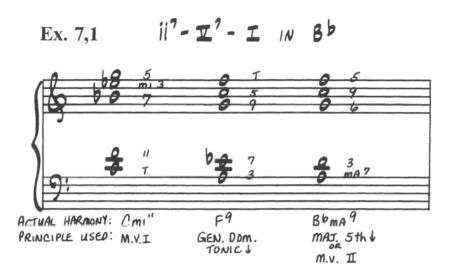

Ex. 7,1 shows generic and miracle voicings employed for a ii7-V7-I in B♭. Let's alter the dominant V7 to include the alteration (♭9). The fraction is $\frac{VI}{I7}$, or in this case F13(♭9).

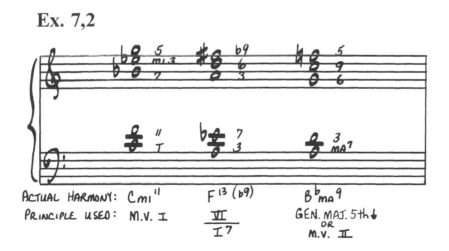

By playing Ex. 7,2, we notice a couple of new favorable tonal bonuses:

1. The voice leading of the soprano voice has more sense of motion and resolution than in Ex. 7,1 due to the descending chromaticism of the line. (This topic of the melodic soprano voice leading will be addressed later in Chapter 11.)

2. The descending parallel triads in second inversion in the right hand create a smooth aural effect, and resolution from the altered V7 to the I sounds more convincing than in Ex. 7,1 because there is more tension in the alteration and no tones common to both harmonies. Hence, the resolution is simply more "resolute".

26   To practice this progression in all keys, the root of the I Major triad becomes the root of the minor ii7 chord. For ex., CMi11 - F13(b9) - BbMa7; BbMi11 - Eb13(b9) - AbMa9; Abmi11 etc. Note that as this sequential progression descends, it will be advisable to supply roots for the dominant V7 and major I in the bottom voice as the right hand thumb dips below middle C.

Ex. 7,3

* BEGINNING WITH THIS BAR WHEN THE RULE OF THUMB IS NO LONGER IN EFFECT TONICS SHOULD BE PLAYED IN THE LEFT HAND AS THE LOWEST VOICE.

Practice the other six keys in similar fashion.

Ex. 7,4

* WHEN VOICINGS DESCEND INTO THE LOWER REGISTER IT'S ADVISABLE TO USE TONICS AS THE LOWEST VOICE IN THE LEFT HAND TO AVOID MUDDY SONOROTIES.

Practice these ii-V7-I's shown in Ex. 7,3 and 7,4 in other randomly selected key sequences. For ex., practice ii11 - V13(♭9) - I in the following sequence: C, E, A♭, B, D, F, A, D♭, E♭, F♯, B♭, G. This insures that the theoretical principles behind the voicings are memorized and that the hands are not reliant on mechanical motor memory.

Ex. 7,5 offers the same progression (ii-V7-I) with the same dominant alteration (♭9), but with a different soprano voice leading.

Ex. 7,5

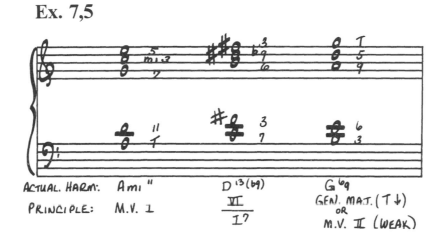

Practice 7,5 in all 12 keys following both a cyclical and random key sequence.

28   Let's try a ii-V7-I with another dominant alteration (#9/#5). Our polychord fraction for this alteration is $\frac{bVI}{I7}$.

Ex. 7,8

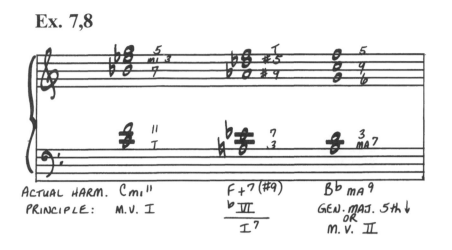

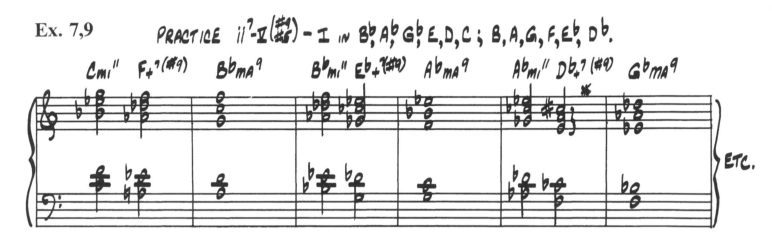

ACTUAL HARM.	Cmi¹¹	F+⁷(#9)	Bbma⁹
PRINCIPLE:	M.V. I	$\frac{bVII}{I^7}$	GEN. MAJ. 5th↓ OR M.V. II

Practice this progression until it is "ingrained". Utilize both a cyclical key sequence (Ex. 7,9) for motor memory, and a random key sequence (Ex. 7,10) for the theoretical assimilation.

Ex. 7,9   PRACTICE ii⁷-V(#9/#5)-I IN Bb, Ab, Gb; E, D, C; B, A, G, F, Eb, Db.

(*) PRACTICE THE PRECEDING PROGRESSION OVER THE RANDOM KEY SEQUENCE: C, E, Ab, B, D, F, A, Db, Eb, F#, Bb, G.

Ex. 7,10

The dominant alteration ($\flat$9/$\flat$5) which is accommodated by the polychord fraction $\frac{\flat V}{I}$ is equally as functional in a ii7-V7-I progression.

Ex. 7,11a   ii⁷-V⁷(♭9♭5)-I   in "G"   ### Ex. 7,11b

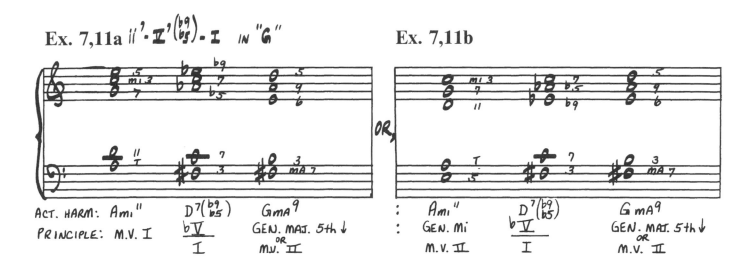

Practice Examples 7,11a and b like the previous examples in this chapter; both over a cyclical and random key sequence.

Cyclical: ii7 - V7($\flat$9/$\flat$5) – I in the following keys: G, F, E$\flat$, D$\flat$, B, A, A$\flat$, G$\flat$, E, D, C, B$\flat$

Random: Invent your own sequence, or use that of Ex. 7,10.

The dominant alterations ($\sharp$9) and ($\sharp$11) could be used in a ii7-V7-I progression as examples 7,12 and 7,13 demonstrate.

Ex. 7,12   ii⁷-V⁷(♯9)-I   in "G"   ### Ex. 7,13   ii⁷-V¹³(♯11)-I   in "G"

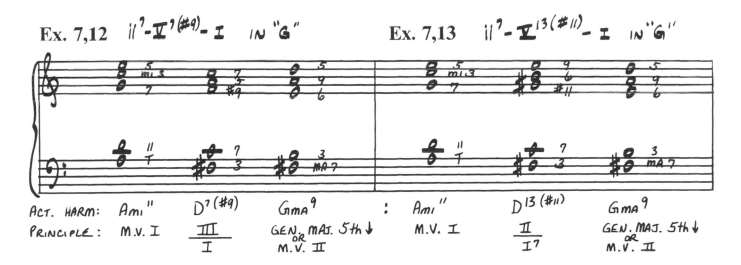

The dominant alterations of ($\sharp$9) and ($\sharp$11) are, however, different from the other alterations in as much as their tonal properties do not require resolution. In other words, the dominant ($\sharp$9) and dominant ($\sharp$11) are (to borrow a baseball analogy) free agents. By the nature of their sonority, they do not require resolution to a tonic, but rather, are self-sufficient harmonies that may function in a tonic capacity themselves. For example, the first chord in Coltrane's **Blue Trane** is the tonic E$\flat$7 with the alteration ($\sharp$9).

Similarly, the suspended dominant or 11th chord is also harmonically independent, and its tonal properties (tensions) do not require a resolution. The negation of this V-I dominant-tonic relationship is evident in the jazz standard **Maiden Voyage** by Herbie Hancock.

In the A section, 4 bars of D9sus are followed by four bars of F9sus. The root movement is obviously not cyclical (V - I), but rather, I - ♭III. The B section begins with a harmony of E♭sus followed by D♭mi11. Again, we don't have a cyclical V - I root relationship, and the "free agent" status of the suspended dominant (11th) chord has been validated.

Another point of interest concerning the suspended dominant chord: the voicing will be identical to that of ii7 voicing in a ii-V7-I progression.

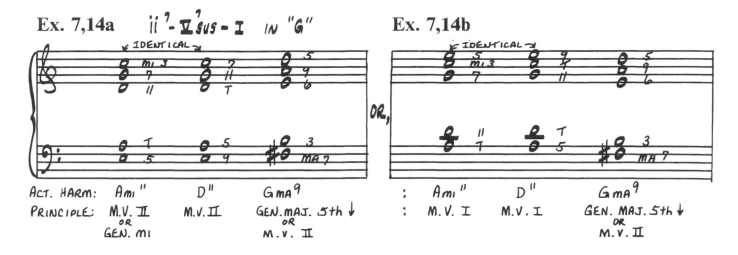

If the principle of minimal motion between adjacent harmonies is observed as in the above examples, the same chord spelling serves two functions, the minor ii, and the suspended dominant V. The bass player would supply the different tonics.

In Summation:

1. Acquaint yourself with the various polychord fractions for the altered and suspended dominants. Devise a method to drill yourself on these fractions until they are automatic.

2. Practice repeatedly the ii7-V7-I progressions shown in this chapter. You will cross paths with ii-V7-I's every day of your musical lives unless you choose to pursue a career of atonal or serial performance. If this be the case, good luck.

3. Remember because of the "tensions" which aurally suggest a resolution, the best alterations for the dominant in the ii7-V7-I progression are:

      a. ♭9 Polychord fractions $\frac{VI}{I7}$

      b. ♭9/♭5 Polychord fraction $\frac{♭V}{I}$

      c. ♯9/♯5 Polychord fraction $\frac{♭VI}{I7}$

The other alterations, ♯9 ($\frac{♭III}{I}$) and ♯11 ($\frac{II}{I7}$) as well as the suspended dominant ($\frac{♭VII}{I}$) may be used. However, the aural sense of tension/resolution between the dominant and the tonic is not as apparent as in the cases of the aforementioned.

Chapter 8: VOICINGS FOR THE BLUES AND OTHER COMMON PROGRESSIONS

Let's now use combinations of Generic Voicings, Miracle Voicings, and Polychord Fractions to voice various blues progressions. We can play the basic blues in "A♭" (three chord progression) with only generic dominants.

Please note that some rhythmic ingenuity must be employed by the jazz pianist with the suggested voicings, rather than simply playing each voicing religiously in each bar on beat one. Comping repeatedly on beat one is one of those unwritten cardinal sins and is guaranteed to annoy your colleagues on the band stand. Listen to the respected masters of the art of comping, e.g. Wynton Kelly, Red Garland, Kenny Drew, Herbie Hancock, to mention a few, in order to familiarize yourself with styllistically correct comping.

Ex. 8,1

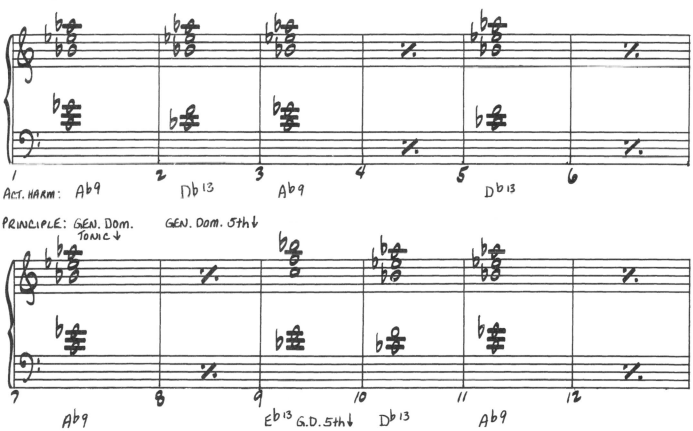

Practice Ex. 8,1 and all subsequent exercises in all twelve keys.

32   Ex. 8,2 is a blues progression in E♭ with more variety than the basic three chord version shown in Ex. 8,1.

Ex. 8,2

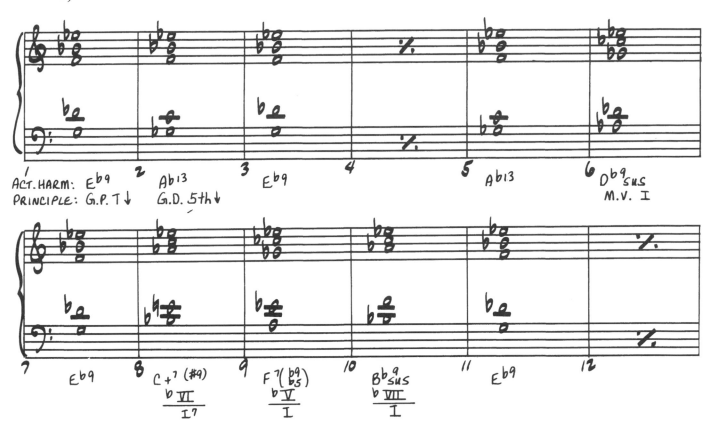

Note that beginning in bar 7 we have the cyclical changes, I - VI - II - V - I - ⁒ with bars 8-10 using altered or suspended dominants. More importantly, notice that the soprano voice remains unchanged (glued) throughout the entire progression.

Ex. 8,3 alters the blues progression even more with alternate II-V's and the "Coltrane turnaround" (I - ♭III - ♭VI - ♭II) in the last two bars.

Ex. 8,3

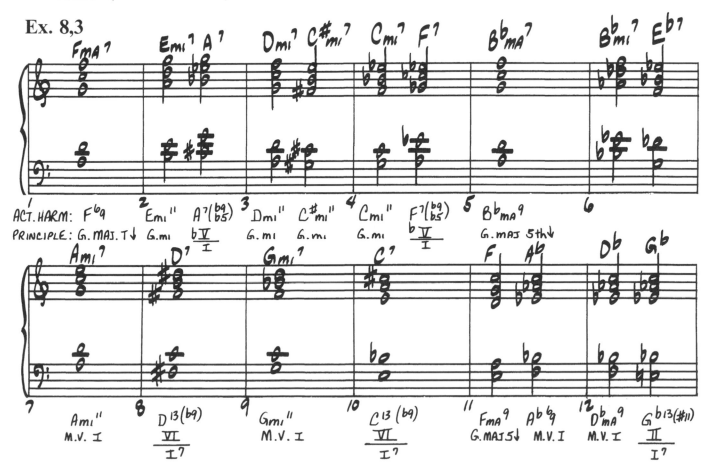

Notice that the voicings of the chords in progression 8,3 move with minimal motion between adjacent harmonies and that the "Rule of Thumb" is in effect. Observe another prerequisite for successful comping: the logical melodic contour of the soprano voice. By tying all identical adjacent soprano notes, we derive the following:

Ex. 8,4

There are numerous other blues progressions. A Dan Haerle handout lists 16 Blues progressions with the footnote "Portions of these progressions could be combined with each other to combine hundreds of slight variations of the above." However, as long as we're aware of minimal motion, "Rule of Thumb", and the new concept of melodic soprano voice leading, there's no ground for anxiety even if there were one million possible blues progressions. We would just simply and logically use our harmonic vocabulary (Generic Voicings, Miracle Voicings, and Polychord Fractions) to accomodate the desired harmonies.

Let's now tackle the project of comping for a tune which doesn't use a blues progression, Tad Dameron's **Ladybyrd**.

Ex. 8,5 "LADYBYRD"

By Tad Dameron

Ex. 8,6 offers a successful way of voicing the chord symbols to **Ladybyrd.**

Bear in mind that songs in lead sheet form, i.e. a single line melody with accompanying chord symbols, generally employ the simplest harmonic possibility for the chord symbol. It is therefore the pianist's option, if not responsibility, to embellish or sophisticate the given harmony. Of course, consideration must be given to the melody. The pianist may add extensions or altered tones only to the extent that they do not clash with the melody.

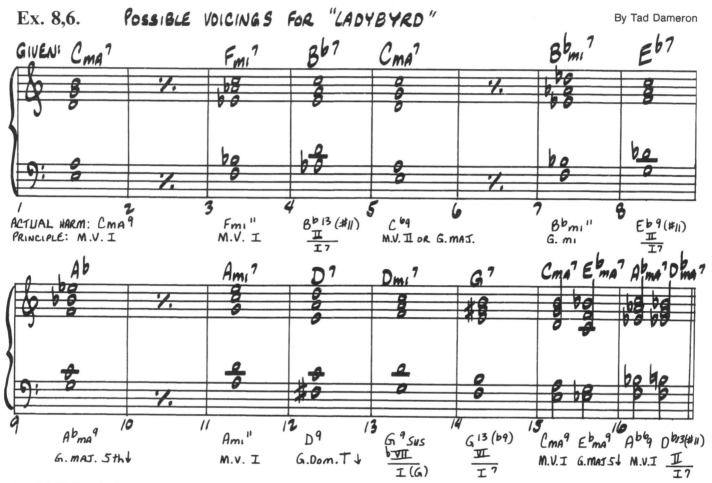

Bar 1: M.V. I in the strong major function with the Ma7th as the soprano voice. Generic major constructions either from the tonic or the fifth descending would have functioned equally as well for the first bar.

Bar 2: ✗.

Bar 3: The M.V. I Fmi11 was obtained by simply moving all 5 voices of the preceding harmony up ½ step.

Bar 4: Referring to bar 4 of Ex. 8,5, we see that the melody lands on the non-diatonic "E", which can either be analyzed as ♭5 or ♯11. Since the chord symbol for this bar (B♭7) is a dominant construction, we can employ the polychord fraction $\frac{II}{I7}$ to accomodate both melody and harmony. II Major triad in the key of B♭ is C Major. Tritone indicators D (3rd) and A♭ (7th) represent the denominator I7.

Bar 5: Simply for variance with bar 1, Generic Major (M.V.II) from the tonic descending supplies a C6/9 in approximation of the desired CMa7.

Bar 6: ✗.

Bar 7: Moving all 5 voices of the Generic Major C6/9 in bar 5-6 up ½ step gives us a close approximation of B♭mi7, B♭mi11.

Bar 8: Refer to Ex. 8,5 to check the melodic symmetry between bars 4 and 8. Again, in bar 8, the melody lights on the #11 while the basic harmony is dominant. The fraction here is $\frac{II}{I7}$ or $\frac{F}{E♭7}$. Tritone indicators (3rd and 7th) suffice for the denominator, E♭7, while the right hands **moves as little as possible** from the preceeding construction in bar 7 to the nearest F Major triad.

Bar 9: Here's the Generic Major construction for the A♭ from the 5th descending. M.V.I (weak major) would have been closer to the previous harmony, but the ever-so-slight jump to M.V.II is justified by the stronger sonority.

Bar 10: ✗.

Bar 11: The closest minor voicing from the previous is M.V.I (Ami11).

Bar 12: D7 is voiced as a Generic Dominant from the tonic descending (D9).

Bar 13: The G9sus (F/G) is the first radical deviation from the original harmony. Rather than have the soprano voice leap from the "D" in the previous bar to an "F" above (Generic Minor construction for Dmi) or to an "A" below (M.V.I minor function), I've opted for the nearest G9sus (F/G) since the ingredients (D, F, A, C, G) of a Dmi11 and a G9sus are identical.

Bar 14: Once again, I've taken the liberty to alter the lead sheet harmony, G7. The main motive behind selecting the alteration (♭9) was twofold: A. The parallel descending motion of the Right hand triad from the previous bar, i.e. F triad to E triad offers a nice tonal effect. B. The polychord fraction $\frac{VI}{I7}$ is a high tension dominant alteration which makes the resolution in the next bar aurally gratifying.

Bar 15: M.V.I as the resolution to the I (C Major, strong function) necessitates the least movement. For the E♭Ma7, I've moved to the nearby Generic Major, 5th descending. As this chord is constructed in a lower (but allowable) register of the keyboard, I've substituted the root for the Major seventh as the lowest voice. This avoids a potential "tonic clash" with the bassist.

Bar 16: M.V.I (weak major function) accommodates the A♭Ma7 while adhering to the "Rule of Thumb". The Polychord $\frac{II}{I7}$ for the altered dominant D♭13 (♯11) offers more tonal tension than a major voicing. However, it would also be possible to keep the M.V.I voicing for the duration of the bar since it functions for both A♭ and D♭ Major.

Obviously, in performance the preceeding bar by bar analysis and execution must happen spontaneously, with no time for deliberation. However, we now have covered all the voicings used in Ex. 8,6 and understand the logic involved in moving from one harmony to the next. Ex. 8,7 supplies the only missing ingredient to make our comping rendition of **Ladybyrd** sound like that of a master: rhythm.

By Tad Dameron

Ex. 8,7   "LADYBYRD"

Practice Ex. 8,7 until it feels natural, or like "you wrote it". Using the same voicings quoted in Ex. 8,6, comp, but with your own rhythms.

Chapter 9: VOICINGS FOR DIMINISHED AND HALF-DIMINISHED SEVENTH CHORDS

The principles of quartal chord construction are obviously impossible to implement with harmonies whose basic intervallic building block is the minor third.

Ex. 9,1a   **b.**

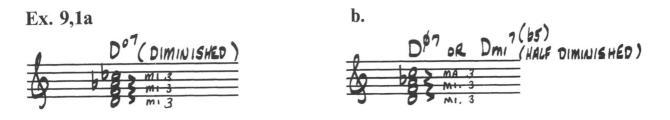

Therefore, a return to third city (tertial construction) is necessary to voice diminished and half-diminished seventh chords. There are, however, ways to restructure these harmonies so that when voiced, the sound is palatable and avoids the strict succession of stacked thirds.

For fully diminished sevenths, an alternative voicing is constructed as follows:

With the tonic note on top, form a major triad in second inversion. Add the tone a tritone lower than bottom voice of the inverted triad to supply a fourth voice. This is a 4-voice construction.

Ex. 9,2

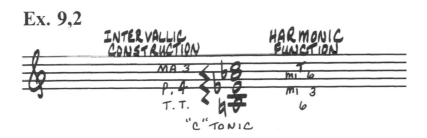

If we consider the top voice of Ex. 9,2 as the tonic, the second voice is indeed a non-chordal tone, having nothing to do with the parent scale, C diminished. It is rather the construction of this chord, i.e., the second inversion major triad over the tritone, plus the presence of both the A and A♭ which gives it a distinctive sonority.

Coincidentally, if analyzed with the tone "F" as the tonic, we have the altered dominant, F7(♯9), or ♭III/I. This construction also serves "B" or "C♭" as a 13(♭9), or VI/I7 .

Ex. 9,3   SAME CONSTRUCTION WITH "F" AS TONIC.

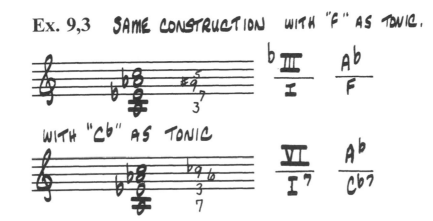

38 How you choose to perceive this chord mathematically or intellectually is, however, not the issue. Simply stated, it sounds good in a diminished context. Let's use this construction in context of a standard tune, Jobim's "Wave".

In example 9,4, I've constructed our diminished voicing (Ex. 9,4) from the "G" descending in the second complete bar, and sequenced this voicing at the interval of a minor third to move parallel with the melody. If tempo should make execution of this bar hazardous or impossible, a simpler solution would be:

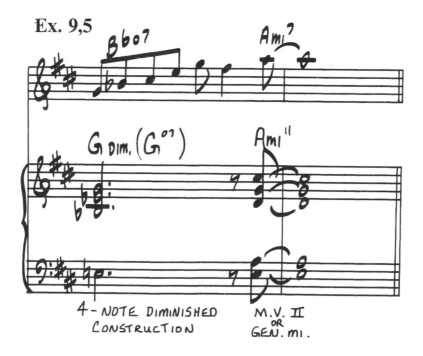

As in the case of strict tertial diminished seventh chords (Ex. 9,1a), our diminished construction can be inverted at the interval of a minor third. In other words, the following diminished constructions patterned after Ex. 9,2 are interchangeable.

$$G^{o7} = B^{\flat o7} = C^{\sharp o7} = E^{o7}$$
$$F^{\sharp o7} = A^{o7} = C^{o7} = E^{\flat o7}$$
$$F^{o7} = A^{\flat o7} = B^{o7} = D^{o7}$$

The sonority of half diminished seventh chords can also be improved by avoiding a strict succession of the thirds. An alternative voicing:

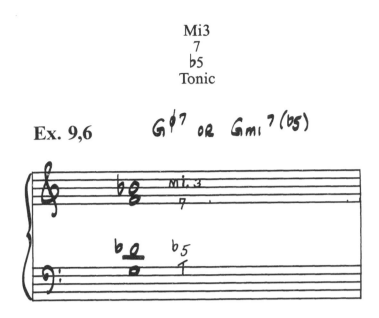

This construction extracts the third from the triad and puts it in the soprano. This spreads out the sonority and avoids stacked thirds.

Another alternative is to voice the G⌀7 as an E♭13 with the tonic omitted. The mathematical relationship is as follows: The tonic of the half diminished chord becomes the third of the dominant 13th.

For example:

A⌀7 could be voiced as a F13 from the 5th descending, generic construction.

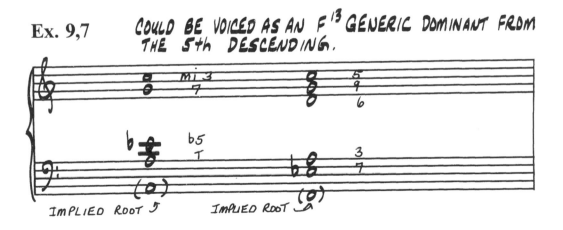

Chapter 10: TRITONE SUBSTITUTIONS AND ½ STEP PREPARATION

As mentioned earlier, the most frequently encountered progression in Western jazz and commercial music is the ii-V-I. As a means of harmonic variance, the V, or dominant harmony, is sometimes replaced or substituted by a harmony constructed on the ♭II scale step. This is known as a tritone substitution since the interval between the root of the V and ♭II harmonies is a tritone.

Ex. 10,1

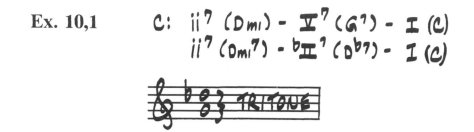

When the root movement between two adjacent harmonies is **not** cyclical (roots ascending in perfect fourths), a similar technique of prefacing a desired harmony from a ½ step above is known as "Half step preparation". For example, in the progression:

$$\frac{4}{4} \ | \ \text{FMa7} \ | \ \text{Ami7} \ \text{A♭7} \ | \ \text{Gmi} \ |$$

we may take the liberty to split the first bar and "prepare" the Ami7 with a dominant harmony based on the root ½ step above. In other words:

$$\text{Fma7} \ \text{B♭13} \ | \ \text{Ami7} \ \text{A♭7} \ | \ \text{Gmi} \ | \qquad \text{is an option.}$$

In instances where tritone substitutions and half step preparation are appropriate, four rules must be held in consideration:

1. Dominants work best as the substituted harmony.

2. The melody (if applicable) will influence the harmony and possible alterations of the substituted chord.

3. The substituted harmony will always resolve to a harmony ½ step lower.

4. If the root movement is cyclical, tritone subs and ½ step preparation are synonymous terms.

Let's take the first 8 bars of "All The Things You Are" for a laboratory experiment with tri-tone substitutions and ½ step preparation.

First, the melody and changes in fake book form:

Ex. 10,2   *"ALL THE THINGS YOU ARE"*

Words by Oscar Hammerstein II
Music by Jerome Kern

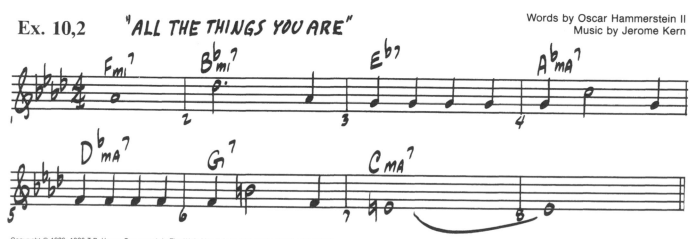

Let's now split each bar with the given harmony for the first two beats, and the substituted harmony for the last two beats. A bar by bar explanation of the theoretical procedures used will be offered after the example.

"ALL THE THINGS YOU ARE"

Words by Oscar Hammerstein II
Music by Jerome Kern

Ex. 10,3

Since our options for the substituted harmony are multiple, we'll denote our choice with an asterisk (*)

Bar 1: Root movement between bars 1 and 2 is cyclical. Therefore, the *B13 is a tritone substitute. The melody "A♭" is the enharmonic "G♯" which is the 13th in relation to the tonic of the substitute, B.

Other possibilities:

1. $B13(\sharp 11) = \frac{II}{I7} = \frac{C\sharp}{B7}$

2. $B13(\flat 9) = \frac{VI}{I7} = \frac{G\sharp}{B7}$

The answer to which of the possibilities is preferable is subjective. Context and your ear are the sole judge and jury of which harmony is appropriate.

Bar 2: Cyclical root movement between bars 2 and 3. Root of tri-tone sub is "E". Chord quality options are:

*1. $E13(\flat 9) = \frac{VI}{I7} = \frac{C\sharp}{E7}$

2. **E13 (unaltered)**

3. $E13(\sharp 11) = \frac{II}{I7} = \frac{F\sharp}{E7}$

Bar 3: Cyclical root movement. Root of tri-tone sub is A. The chosen possibility for the chord quality, *A7(♭9/♭5) creates maximum tension and makes resolution to the AbMa7 tonally gratifying. Other possibilities:

1. $A9sus = \frac{\flat VII}{I} = \frac{G}{A}$

2. $A7(\sharp 9) = \frac{\flat III}{I} = \frac{C}{A}$

3. **A7(♭5)** (tertially constructed)

4. **A7(♭9)** (tertially constructed)

Bar 4: Cyclical root movement. Root of tritone sub is "D". Possibilities are:

*1. $D7(\flat 9/\flat 5) = \frac{\flat V}{I} = \frac{Ab}{D}$

2. $D9sus = \frac{\flat VII}{I} = \frac{C}{D}$

3. $D7(\sharp 9) = \frac{\flat III}{I} = \frac{F}{D}$

4. **D7** (tertially constructed)

Bar 5: Root movement from "D♭" to the following "G" is a tritone, not cyclical. Therefore half step preparation is in order. A♭ is obviously the tonic of the substituted harmony while the "F" melody note implies a 13th. Options are:

1. **A♭13**

2. $Ab13(\flat 9) = \frac{VI}{I7} = \frac{F}{Ab7}$

*3. $Ab13(\sharp 11) = \frac{II}{I7} = \frac{Bb}{Ab7}$

Bar 6: Tritone sub on "D♭". "B" on beat 3 allows many chord quality possibilities:

1. **D♭7** with all optional alterations (♭5, ♯5, ♭9, ♯9)

*2. $Db7(\flat 9/\flat 5) = \frac{\flat V}{I} = \frac{G}{Db}$

3. $Db7(\sharp 9) = \frac{\flat III}{I} = \frac{E}{Db}$

4. $Db7sus = \frac{\flat VIII}{I} = \frac{Cb}{Db}$

Because the harmony of bar 7 is the same as bar 8, half step preparation and return seemed redundant and inappropriate.

To determine whether or not a polychord fraction could be used, in a particular situation, use the following procedure:

The melody note which is either sounded on beat 3, or previously sounded and held over beat 3 is a participant chord tone in each of three major triads. To facilitate the explanation of this, let's analyze measure #3 of Ex. 10,3.

Ex. 10,4

The melody note on beat 3 is "G". "G" is a member of 3 major triads.

    a. the tonic of G major triad
    b. the third of E♭ major triad
    c. the fifth of C major triad

Now, we determine:

Which of these three major triads can be used as the numerator for a polychord fraction with A7 as the denominator.

    a. G/A is the polychord fraction $\frac{\flat VII}{I}$ A9sus

    b. E♭/A is the polychord fraction $\frac{\flat V}{I}$ A7(♭9/♭5)

    c. C/A is the polychord fraction $\frac{\flat III}{I}$ A7(♯9)

Consequently, all the above are possibilities. Which harmony we select is simply a matter of taste. When multiple possibilities are available, influencing factors are the preceeding and subsequent harmonies. The sole judge of which harmony is ultimately chosen is your ear.

Having examined the options, and theoretically justifying our choices for tritone subs and ½ step preparation harmonies, let's now voice Ex. 10,3.

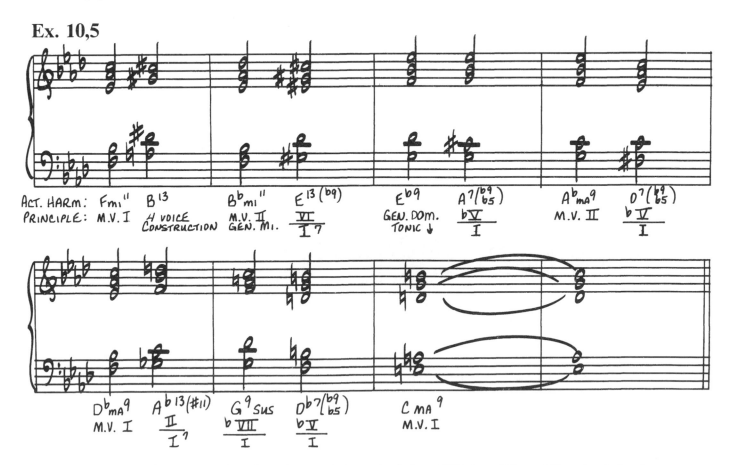

Ex. 10,5

As in all previous examples, I've observed the principles of "Rule of Thumb" and minimal motion between adjacent harmonies.

Chapter 11: THE MELODIC SOPRANO VOICE
(Melodic Comping)

As previously mentioned, if the top voice of each chord construction progresses to the next top voice in some logical sequence, preferably diatonically or chromatically, your comping will have a sense of fluidity and continuity. "Melodic comping" emphasizes the logic and musicality of your chord choices by devoting attention to the voice leading of the soprano or top voice of the adjacent harmonies in the progression.

Sample progression #1   Gmi7 | C7(b9) | FMa7 | C7sus

This progression is the frequently encountered ii - V - I in "F" with a return to the V7sus. It could be voiced in the following fashion:

Ex. 11,1

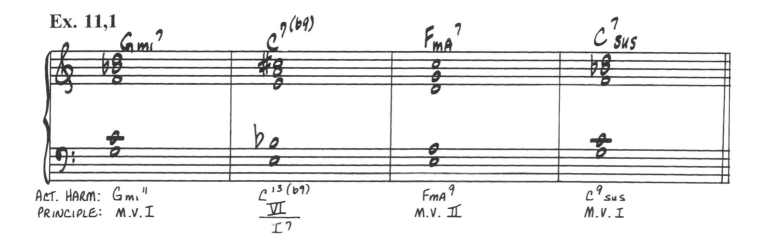

Analyzing Ex. 11,1, we must consent to chord quality approximations like the Gmi11 for the desired Gmi7. The harmony is, in effect, enhanced by the addition of the 11th.

The voicing for the C7(b9) is the polychord fraction $\frac{VI}{I7}$ using tritone indicators for the denominator. In bar 3, the FMa7 is voiced as a generic major FMa9 descending from the 5th scale tone.

Although implying a different root, the voicing for the C7sus in bar 4 is Miracle Voicing I and identical to the Gmi11 in bar 1.

The voice leading of the soprano voice follows a simple logic.

Ex. 11,2

So, now we have three criterion to successful voicing:

1. The "Rule of Thumb"

2. Minimal motion between adjacent harmonies, and

3. Melodic soprano voice leading

A critic would be quick to point out that the criterion #2 "minimal motion" would ensure melodic soprano voice leading, or that they are interchangeable (One presupposes the other). This is not true in every instance. Occasionally, the minimal motion concept will take a back seat to melodic soprano voice leading if the result is more musically interesting.

To demonstrate, let's take sample progression #2 and voice it.

Sample progression #2:   EbMa7 | Ab9(#11) | Fmi7 | Bb7 | EbMa7

Ex. 11,3 (Voicing of sample progression #2)

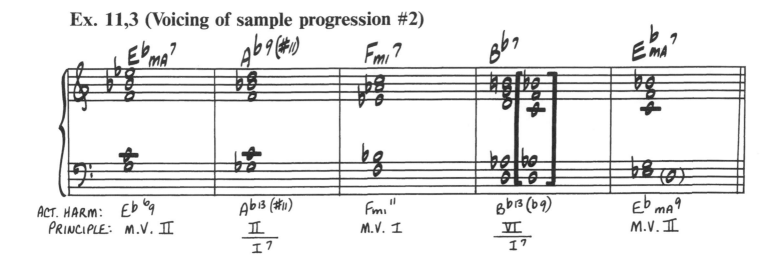

In bar 4, I've taken the liberty to alter the given Bb7 harmony to a dominant (b9) in order to create a stronger melodic line in the soprano voice. In this instance, the "minimal motion" concept has been sacrificed to allow a smooth melodic line.

Ex. 11,4

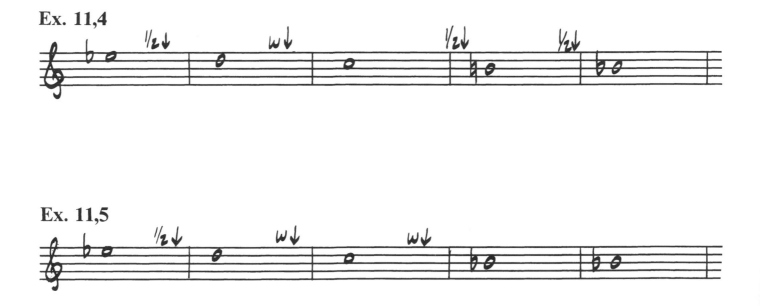

Ex. 11,5

The soprano voice leading in example 11,4 has both more sense of motion and resolution than does the voice leading Ex. 11,5 where the soprano voice remains stationary between bars 4 and 5.

Simply stated, the voice leading in example 11,4 favors the melodic soprano voice leading concept, whereas Ex. 11,5 places the "minimal motion" concept in higher priority.

Both are correct and once again, only taste and context would determine which should be used.

Chapter 12: SAMPLE PROGRESSIONS FOR FURTHER STUDY

Excerpts of two standard tunes in lead sheet form (melody and chord symbols) are printed below for harmonization (voicing). Voice these excerpts using the given harmonies and the techniques you've learned in the previous chapters:

- a. Generic Voicings
- b. Miracle Voicings
- c. Polychord Fractions

While harmonizing each lead sheet example, consider employing the various methods of alteration previously discussed:

- a. Tri-tone substitutions
- b. Half step preparation
- c. Altered dominants via Polychords

Following each excerpt, the author will present and discuss a possible voicing solution. Bear in mind, there is simply no one single definitive approach to correct voicings. Ways to voice chords are as diverse as the pianists who voice them. To illustrate, imagine the renditions of the same chord progression by two pianists, Oscar Peterson and Chick Corea. Both would be correct although stylistically different.

With respect for the melody and the basic harmonic motion, Ex. 12,1 ("Pennies From Heaven") could be voiced in the following manner. Three staves are used; the top is Ex. 12,1 and the bottom two are the "realization" in basic rhythmic values:

Bar by Bar Analysis:

Bar 1: With C6 belonging to the Major family and the first melody note being "C" the obvious choice came to mind, C6/9 voiced as a Generic Major T↓ (or M.V. II.).

The F13 on the second half of the bar is an obvious deviation from the Emi in the original. However, the melody is acknowledged and the F13 sets up a nice chromatically descending line in the bass from IV (F13) to ii (Dmi11) in bar 3.

Bar 2: Emi11 voiced as a M.V.I is the obvious choice to follow the F13 which preceeded in bar 1. It accomodates the melody, harmonic motion, and chromatically descending bass line. The D#°7 or B7 (♭9)/D# chromatically sets up the Dmi11 in bar 3, one of the focal harmonies.

Bar 3: Minimal motion to M.V. I as a D minor function is the obvious choice.

Bar 4: The movement of the F Major triad in 2nd inversion (R.H. bar 3) to the Emi triad and 2nd inversion (R.H. bar 4) gives a nice parallel aural effect. In the left hand, the tenor voice moves parallel with the R.H. triads while the bass covers the tonics.

Bar 5: Surprise! Here's a tritone substitution of F#ø7 [F#Mi7(b5)] to continue a chromatically descending bass line beginning with the "G" in bar 4. The half diminished tritone as a substitute for the tonic Major was a harmonic device favored by Bill Evans and others of his era.

Minimal motion to the nearest M.V. I for Fmi11 heeds both the melody and the motion of the chromatic bass line.

Bar 6: If we moved all voices down a half step from the Fmi11 in bar 5 we have M.V. I as an Emi function. I've moved the top voice from "B" to "D" simply to reinforce the melody.

The A13 acknowledges the melody and cyclically sets up the ii7 (Dmi11) that's to come in bar 7. The cyclical progression iii7 (Emi11) — VI7 (A13) — ii (Dmi11). The voicing of the A13 is similar to the Generic Dominant 5↓. However, the soprano voice "E" has been deleted and the tonic has been added on the bottom. This construction supports the stated melody, is basically quartal, and the soprano offers a nice melodic line from the previous harmony and to the following harmony.

Bar 7: Minimal motion takes us to the nearest Dmi, M.V.I. The top three voices (F triad in 2nd inversion) are now going to conveniently contribute to the two subsequent harmonies as polychords: $\frac{VI}{I7}$ on an Ab root offers a tritone sub for the Dmi resolving to a G9sus voiced as a $\frac{bVII}{I}$ in bar 8.

Before we take a look at another sample progression, keep in mind that in a real life comping situation, it may be the soloist's preference that you not comp with the melody note in the soprano of your chord constructions. Professional singers have a particular aversion to this practice. If the pianist's voicings do not favor the melody constantly, the singer (or other soloist) has considerably more melodic freedom and flexibility. Also, intonation becomes a more critical issue if the pianist voices all chords with the melody note in the soprano.

Let's look now at Ex. 12,3, a lead sheet version of the first eight bars of Rodger's and Hart's "The Lady Is A Tramp."

Ex. 12,3   "THE LADY IS A TRAMP"

Words by Lorenz Hart
Music by Richard Rodgers

Having mentioned that it is not always desirable to voice chords strictly with the melody note as the soprano voice, I'm offering two solutions: Ex. 12,4 pays fairly stringent respect to the melody by offering voicings with the melody primarily in the top voice. Ex. 12,5 (the singer's version) accommodates the harmonic motion while avoiding doubling the melody in the soprano voice.

Ex. 12,4 "THE LADY IS A TRAMP"

Words by Lorenz Hart
Music by Richard Rodgers

Bar by Bar Analysis of Ex. 12,4:.

Bar 1: A C6/9 is voiced as a M.V.II. or Generic Major from the tonic descending.

Bar 2: Eb7(#9) voiced as a $\frac{\flat III}{I}$ has been substituted for the original Cmi7. This changes the tonic from the "C" in bar 1 to an "Eb" rather than remain stationary. The melody is in the top voice.

Bar 3: Moving the preceeding harmony down a half step gives us obviously a D7(#9). On beat 4, I've substituted the dominant "G" with the tritone substitution, Db7(b9/b5). A sixth voice, the tonic, has been added to guarantee that the upper five voices are not mistaken as a G7.

Bar 4: ∕.

Bar 5: Minimal motion takes us to the nearest C Major construction, Generic Major, from the tonic descending.

Bar 6: Here I've used the same numerator triad as in bar 2, Gb Major in 2nd inversion. This time, however, over the VI scale step with a resultant harmony of A13 (b9).

Bar 7: Descending numerator triads from Gb in bar 5 to F in bar 6 enables a smooth transition to M.V.I. for the Dmi11.

Bar 8: Moving the numerator triad again down a half step to E, we set up the dominant polychord, $\frac{VI}{I7}$ for a compact G13(b9). "B" was added on top as a melody reinforcement.

Ex. 12,5 is an equally valid "realization", but with no emphasis on having the melody note as the top voice of each chord.

Ex. 12,5 "THE LADY IS A TRAMP"

Words by Lorenz Hart
Music by Richard Rodgers

Bar by Bar Analysis of Ex. 12,5:

Bar 1: C Major voiced generically from the 5th descending is as good an opener as any.

Bar 2: The E♭9, voiced as a Generic Dominant (T↓), prepares the upcoming Dmi harmony and doesn't clash with the melody.

Bar 3: Another surprise! A tertial spelling of a Dmi9. Why?

a. Voice leading from the preceeding harmony was optimally smooth, and,

b. The tertial voicing of the DMi9 offers a pleasant aural contrast to the previous voicings which were predominantly quartal.

Note, however, that the chord is not voiced **as a strict succession of thirds.**

Bar 4: Tied over from bar 3 is G7(♭9/♭5) $\frac{♭V}{I}$ which was quite accessible to our Dmi9. Both the G7(♭9/♭5) and the following unaltered G9 do not aggravate the melody note "B".

Bars 5-8 exemplify the concept of melodic comping. Note that the soprano voice has enough motion to even be considered a counter melody. However, the altered harmonies and counter melody function totally as an accompanying duet to the original melody.

Bar 5: The bottom voice of the Generic Minor construction for Emi has simply been lobbed off leaving us a 4-voice quartal construction, still sufficient for Emi11.

Bar 6: The melodic soprano sets up the polychord fraction $\frac{VI}{I7}$ on "A" or A13 (♭9).

Bar 7: The active soprano voice returns to a 4-voice quartal construction for Dmi11.

Bar 8: Bars 7 and 8 are a transposed version of bars 5 and 6. The soprano sets up another 13(♭9), this time constructed on "G".

Obviously, there are many possible solutions to the voicing of any lead sheet melody. May I suggest on first reading that you pay homage to the composers original harmonic intentions before you investigate possibilities for alteration.

Chapter 13: GLOSSARY

Alteration – The individual notes which chromatically deviate from an established diatonic system. For example, in the case of a CMa7(#11), the parenthetical (#11) implies a chromatic **alteration** or deviation from the C Major scale.

Altered – A harmony containing chromatically raised or lowered tones which deviate from an established diatonic system.

Comp – Originally, an abbreviation of the verb complement (Merriam-Webster: to supply a lack). To "complement" in a musical performance by providing harmonic support (chords) preferably in a tasteful, appropriate manner. For ex., "Tommy comped nicely behind the trombone solo."

Comping – to comp.

Diatonic – Adhering to the scale or mode applicable to a given harmony. For ex., Mixolydian is the relevant diatonic system for dominant family chords.

Generic Voicings – Easy to construct 5-note chord constructions which accommodate the three basic families: Major, minor, and dominant. (see Chapter 2)

Miracle Voicings – 5-note chord constructions each with five different harmonic functions. (see Chapter 4)

M.V. – Abbreviation for "Miracle Voicing."

R.H. – Abbreviation for "right hand."

L.H. – Abbreviation for "left hand."

Tertial – Constructed of thirds. A harmonic construction where the major or minor third is the basic intervallic building block. The Harvard Dictionary of Music defines this means of construction as tertially, adv., constructed of thirds "tertian."

Tertiality – Harmonies (chords) constructed essentially of major or minor thirds. In contrast to quartal harmony which is predominantly constructed of perfect fourths.

Quartal – Constructed of fourths. A harmonic construction where the perfect fourth is the basic intervallic building block.

Root – Tonic. Beginning tone of any diatonic system.

Tonic – Root. Beginning tone of any diatonic system.

T↓ – From the tonic descending.

5↓ – From the fifth descending.

"Third City" – Reference to tertially constructed harmonies.

Tritone Indicators – The third and dominant 7th scale tones of a given dominant tonality. These two tones are the strongest tonal indicators of dominant family harmonies. The interval between these two tones is a tritone.

Voicings – a combination of two or more tones sounded simultaneously to accommodate a specified harmony.

Chapter 14: SUGGESTED LISTENING

One of the more memorable quotes I've heard was passed on to me by friend and piano teacher nonpareil, Don Walker of Dekalb, Illinois:

"We all rest on the shoulders of those who precede us."

It would be blatant naivete to assume otherwise. The "current" accomplishments and innovations in music, as well as those in any academic discipline, are only possible as a result of a series of previous milestones achieved by the innovators of previous generations. As Galileo's accomplishments paved the way for those of Einstein, we must correlate that Bach influenced Beethoven; Chopin, Debussy; Art Tatum, Keith Jarrett. Perhaps scientific achievements are more tangibly linked to the past than artistic achievements; however, the dependence is equally undeniable, although the influence is perhaps more subtle and indirect.

Listed below are thirty-five keyboardists whose comping style and chord voicings have influenced this book. These artists have served and will serve as stylistic role models for subsequent generations of jazz keyboardists. Following the name of each "comper," a single recording is listed which exemplifies that individual's comping style. In the interest of brevity, only one recording per artist has been listed. Those below have been listed for their reputations as "compers," not for excellence in other areas such as solo playing, or for their contribution to the heritage of jazz pianism.

The leader's name will be underlined if the keyboardist was not the leader on that particular recording date.

Respected "Compers" (alphabetical listing)

1. Richie Beirach, "Forgotten Fantasies", A & M Records, (SP-709) w. David Liebman (sax)

2. Paul Bley, "Sonny Meets Hawk", RCA 741074/075 w. <u>Sonny Rollins</u> (sax), <u>Coleman Hawkins</u> (sax) Roy McCurdy (dr), Henry Grimes or Bob Cranshaw (b)

3. Joanne Brackeen, "Prism", Choice Records 1024 w. Eddie Gomez (b)

4. Jaki Byard, "Outward Bound", Prestige 7311 w. <u>Eric Dolphy</u> (sax), Freddie Hubbard (tpt), George Tucker (b), Roy Haynes (dr)

5. George Cables, "Cable's Vision", Contemporary 14001, w. Ernie Watts (sax), Freddie Hubbard (tpt), Bobby Hutcherson (vibes), Tony Dumas (b), Peter Erskine (dr)

6. Chick Corea, "Friends", Polydor 1-6160 w. Joe Farrell (ww), Eddie Gomez (b), Steve Gadd (dr)

7. Kenny Drew, "Jackie's Bag", Blue Note 84051 w. <u>Jackie McLean</u> (sax), Blue Mitchell (tpt), Tina Brooks (sax), Paul Chambers (b), Art Taylor (dr)

8. Bill Evans, "Kind Of Blue", Columbia CS 8163 w. <u>Miles Davis</u> (tpt), Cannonball Adderley (sax), John Coltrane (sax), Paul Chambers (b), Jimmy Cobb (dr)

9. Tommy Flanagan, "Kenny Burrell with John Coltrane", Prestige P-24059 w. <u>John Coltrane</u> (sax), Kenny Burrell (g), Paul Chambers (b), Jimmy Cobb (dr)

10. Hal Galper, "Speak With A Single Voice", Century w. Michael Brecker (sax), Randy Brecker (tpt), Wayne Dockery (b), Bob Moses (dr)

11. Red Garland, "Relaxin' With The Miles Davis Quintet", Prestige 7129 w. <u>Miles Davis</u> (tpt), John Coltrane (sax), Paul Chambers (b), Jimmy Cobb (dr)

12. Don Grolnick, "Step By Step", Nippon Columbia YF-7020-N <u>Steps Ahead</u>: Michael Brecker (sax), Mike Mainieri (vibes), Eddie Gomez (b), Steve Gadd (dr)

13. Herbie Hancock, "Maiden Voyage", Blue Note 84195 w. George Coleman (sax), Freddie Hubbard (tpt), Ron Carter (b), Tony Williams (dr)

14. Roland Hanna, "Dear John C.", Impulse A-88 w. Elvin Jones (dr), Richard Davis (b), Charlie Mariano (sax)

15. Barry Harris, "Tune-Up!" Cobblestone 9013 w/ Sonny Stitt (sax), Sam Jones (b), Alan Dawson (dr)

16. Hampton Hawes, "The Seance" Contemporary S7621 w. Red Mitchell (b), Donald Bailey (dr)

17. John Hicks, "Now It's My Turn", Roulette SR-5005 w. Betty Carter (voc), Walter Booker (b), Chip Lyles (dr)

18. Ahmad Jamal, "Ahmad Jamal's Alhambra" Argo 685 w. Israel Crosby (b), Vernell Fournier (dr)

19. Keith Jarrett, "The Survivor's Suite" ECM-1-1085 w. Dewey Redman (sax), Charlie Haden (b), Paul Motian (dr)

20. Hank Jones, "New Wine In Old Bottles" Inner City 6029 w. Jackie McLean (sax) Ron Carter (b), Tony Williams (dr)

21. Wynton Kelly, "Miles Davis In Person Friday Night At The Blackhawk" (Vol. 1) Columbia LE 10018 w. Miles Davis (tpt), Hank Mobley (sax), Paul Chambers (b), Philly Joe Jones (dr)

22. Kenny Kirkland, "Think Of One", Columbia 38641 w. Wynton Marsalis (tpt), Branford Marsalis (sax), Jeffrey Watts (dr), Phil Bowler or Ray Drummond (b)

23. John Lewis, "M.J.Q./Blues At Carnegie Hall", Atlantic SD 1468 w. Milt Jackson (vibes), Percy Heath (b), Connie Kay (dr)

24. Lyle Mays, "Pat Metheny Group" ECM1-1114 w. Pat Metheny (g), Mark Egan (b), Danny Gottlieb (dr)

25. Jim McNeely, "The Plot Thickens", Gatemouth 1001 w. John Scofield (g), Billy Hart (dr), John Burr or Mike Richmond (b)

26. Thelonius Monk, "Thelonius Monk At The Five Spot" Milestone M 47043 w. Johnny Griffin (sax), Ahmed Abdul-Malik (b), Roy Haynes (dr)

27. Oscar Peterson, "Ella & Louis" Verve V6-4003 w. Ella Fitzgerald (voc), Louis Armstrong (tpt & voc), Herb Ellis (g), Ray Brown (b), Louis Bellson or Buddy Rich (dr)

28. Bud Powell, "Charlie Parker's All-Stars 1950", Alamac QSR-2430 w. Charlie Parker (sax), Fats Navarro (tpt), Curley Russell (b), Art Blakey (dr)

29. Horace Silver, "Blowin' The Blues Away", Blue Note 4017 w. Blue Mitchell (tpt), Junior Cook (sax), Eugene Taylor (b), Louis Hayes (dr)

30. Lennie Tristano, "Subconscious-Lee", Prestige 7250 w. Lee Konitz. Other personnel not listed.

31. McCoy Tyner, "Coltrane Live At Birdland", MCA/Impulse 29015 w. John Coltrane (sax), Jimmy Garrison (b), Elvin Jones (dr)

32. Cedar Walton, "Eastern Rebellion 2". Timeless SJP-106 w. Bob Berg (sax), Sam Jones (b), Billy Higgins (dr)

33. James Williams, "Everything I Love", Concord CJ-104 w. Bill Pierce (ww), Dennis Irwin (b), Billy Hart (dr)

34. Joe Zawinul, "Mercy, Mercy, Mercy", Capitol ST 2663 w. Cannonball Adderley (sax), Nat Adderley (tpt), Vic Gatsky (b), Roy McCurdy (dr)

35. Denny Zeitlin, "Tidalwave", Palo Alto 8044-N w. John Abercrombie (g), Charlie Haden (b), Peter Donald (dr)

Chapter 15: A SEMESTER'S SYLLABUS

For those interested in incorporating the preceding material into a semester's Jazz Keyboard Lab, the following 17-week syllabus has been designed. Each week's material covers four crucial areas:

1. The Theoretical. Explanation of the theories and principles of each concept. (e.g. Explaining the theories behind Miracle Voicings)

2. Application of the Theoretical. The playing at the keyboard of the previously discussed concepts.

3. Sight reading. (A must for any novice pianist or doubler). Sight reading benefits eye to hand coordination, technical independence of the hands, and heightens harmonic and contrapuntal awareness. Sight reading materials will depend on the general capability level of the class. To be recommended for independence of the hands and introduction to various modes, Bartok's **Microcosmos** Vol. 1-6 are excellent. These are progressive pieces with Volume 1 being the easiest, Volume 6, the most difficult. Four-handed duets for two pianos are always fun for students to play. Duets are beneficial as an introduction to ensemble playing (playing with others) and for developing an internal pulse or sense of time. Again, the teacher should select duet material difficult enough to challenge but not discourage the class. There are numerous 4-hand duets written for all technical levels and available from your print music dealer.

4. Listening. Never underestimate the constructive value of listening to the masters. Chapter 14 offers a suggested listening list should the teacher need ideas.

Week 1

A. Theoretical. Read and explain the **Foreword** and Chapter 1, **An Overview Of Traditional Jazz harmony.**

B. Application. Play all examples in Chapter 1 to review scales and tertial harmony.

C. Sight Reading and Listening

D. Assignment: Read Chapter 2, **Generic Voicings.**

Week 2

A. Theoretical. Explain Chapter 2, **Generic Voicings** (Major, Minor, and Dominant).

B. Application. Play all examples in Chapter 2.

C. Sight Reading and Listening

D. Assignment. Require students to write two simple one-measure patterns in 4/4 using the notes of the C Major scale and starting on the tonic. For example,

Ex. 15,1   **Ex. 15,2**

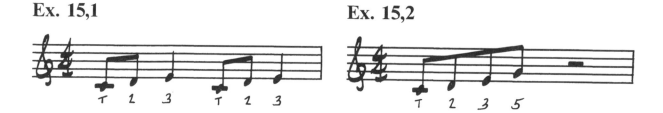

A. Theoretical.

1. Write on blackboard sample patterns brought in by the students. Four or five should suffice.

2. Show students how to alter these patterns by lowering the third scale step in order to accommodate minor harmonies.

Ex. 15,3

Ex. 15,3 is 15,2 altered to accommodate minor harmonies.

B. Application

1. Have class play all the selected sample patterns, both Major and Minor.

2. Play major patterns as dominant patterns by lowering the seventh (if the seventh is present).

3. Divide the class into two groups (A & B).

4. Have group A comp generic cyclical dominants as in Ex.2,14 with a stylistically suitable rhythm. For example,

Ex. 15,4

Simultaneously, group B should play patterns (both hands, please!) over these cyclical dominants. For example, while A group plays 15,4, B group could be playing 15,5.

Ex. 15,5

The teacher at the same time could supply a simple bass line connecting the two harmonies.

Ex. 15,6

5. Transpose these patterns to other keys.

6. Swap. Same procedure, except now group B comps while group A plays the patterns. Teacher continues to hold it together by "walking" bass lines.

C. Sight Reading and Listening

D. Assignment

1. Request that the students start a "Patterns Notebook" by adding those on the board to their own.

2. Bring in two more one-measure major patterns in starting on the third. For example,

Ex. 15,7

Ex. 15,8

3. Read Chapter 3, **Generic Voicings Workout.**

Week 4

A. Theoretical.

1. Dissect Chapter 3 stressing "minimal motion."

2. Put a few random new patterns on the board.

B. Application.

1. Students: Play Ex. 3,1 in all twelve keys.

2. Teacher: Add a walking bass line to perform Ex. 3,1 in time. The following would suffice:

3. Transpose to other keys.

4. Class: Play through randomly selected new patterns beginning on the third. Practice both Major and minor by lowering thirds and sevenths as necessary.

5. Group A: patterns over the ii-V7-I progression; Group B: comp. Teacher: Bass lines.

6. Groups A and B: Swap.

C. Sight Reading and Listening.

D. Assignment.

1. Practice examples 3,2-6. Students should concentrate on "minimal motion" and the "Rule of Thumb." Check voicings with those printed on p.16.

2. Add new patterns to notebook.

Week 5

A. Theoretical. Answer questions pertaining to any previous material.

B. Application.

1. Class: Play 3,2-3,6.

2. Transpose each exercise 3,2-3,6 to a closely related key.

3. Group A, comp to 3,2-3,6, Group B, patterns. Teacher: Walk bass lines.

4. Groups A and B, Swap.

C. Sight Reading and Listening.

D. Assignment: Read Chapter 4, **Miracle Voicings.**

Week 6

A. Theoretical. Discuss and demonstrate the five Assignment harmonic functions of each Miracle Voicing (See Chapter 4).

B. Application.

1. Play Examples 4,2 and 4,4 to acquaint students with Miracle Voicings and their various functions.

2. Review Chapter 3, **Generic Voicings** by transposing 3,2-3,6 to new keys.

3. In these keys: Group A, Patterns; Group B, Comp; Teacher, bass lines.

4. Groups A and B, Swap.

C. Sight Reading and Listening.

D. Assignment. Look over Chapter 5, **Workout With Generic and Miracle Voicings.**

Week 7

A. Theoretical. Using example 5,1, show how Generic and Miracle Voicings can accommodate the chord progression and adhere to the "Rule of Thumb."

B. Application.

1. Practice Examples 5,1-5 slowly. Stress the minimal voice leading between harmonies.

C. Sight Reading and Listening

D. Assignment. Write out voicings on a grand staff to Examples 5,1-5,6.

Week 8

A. Theoretical. Check voicings assignment from previous week with the supplied voicings to 5,1-5,6. Discuss, if any questions.

B. Application

1. Group A, Comp to Examples 5,1-5,6; Group B, Patterns; Teacher, bass lines.

2. Groups A and B, Swap.

C. Sight Reading and Listening

D. Assignment: Write out two one-measure patterns in 4/4 time (C Major) which begin on the fifth scale step. For example,

Ex. 15,10

Ex. 15,11

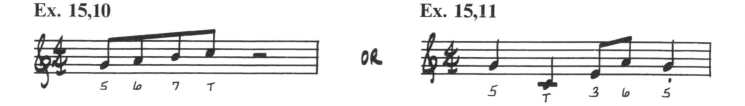

A. Theoretical.

1. Answer any questions pertaining to previous material.

2. Put a few random patterns (beginning on the fifth) on the board.

B. Application

1. Play the new patterns as one would over Major, Minor and Dominant harmonies by altering the third and seventh accordingly.

2. Transpose 5,1-5,6 to closely related keys.

3. In new keys, Group A comps while Group B plays the new patterns with both hands.

4. Swap.

C. Sight Reading and Listening

D. Assignment

1. Read and **comprehend** Chapters 6 and 7.

2. Put new patterns in notebook.

Week 10

A. Theoretical. Today's class time may be predominantly absorbed by theoretical discussion and explanation of Polychord Fractions and their applications. However, it is imperative that these are thoroughly explained and understood.

B. Application.

1. Play through all examples in Chapter 6, **Voicing Suspended and Altered Dominants as Polychord Fractions.** Practice the Polychord Fractions in other keys.

2. Play through the exercise in Chapter 7, **Application of Polychord Fractions In The ii7-V7-I Progression.**

C. Sight Reading and Listening.

D. Assignment.

1. Practice ii7-V7-I with the following alterations for the dominant: $\flat 9$, $\sharp 9/\sharp 5$ and $\flat 9/\flat 5$ in a cyclical key sequence (See 7,3).

2. Practice same over a random key sequence. Invent your own or use that of Ex. 7,10.

3. Read Chapter 8, **Voicings For The Blues And Other Common Progressions.**

Week 11

A. Theoretical. Thoroughly discuss and answer questions pertinent to Chapter 8.

B. Application.

1. Play all examples in Chapter 8.

2. Write three sample patterns on the board (one beginning on the tonic; one, on the third; and, one, on the fifth). Play these Major and minor.

3. Group A, comp to 8,2; Group B, Patterns; Teacher, bass lines.

4. Same procedure for Ex. 8,3.

5. Swap and repeat 3 and 4.

C. Sight Reading and Listening.

D. Assignment. Read Chapter 9, **Voicings For Diminished and Half Diminished Chords.**

Week 12

A. Theoretical. Discuss and answer pertinent to Chapter IX.

B. Application.

1. Play through all examples in Chapter 9.

2. Put random patterns on board. Group A, comp to 8,6, **Ladybyrd.** Group B, play patterns over the chord progression to 8,6.

3. Swap.

C. Sight Reading and Listening.

D. Read Chapter 10, **Tritone Substitutions and Half Step Preparation.**

Week 13

A. Theoretical. Discuss and answer questions pertinent to Chapter 10. This may monopolize the time allotted to the class period.

B. Application.

1. Play through all examples in Chapter 10.

2. Put random patterns on the board. Group A, comp to 10,5, **All The Things You Are.** Group B, play patterns to same.

3. Swap.

4. Put Blues progression on board with some altered dominants.

5. Class: comp to progression while individuals improvise with or without regard to patterns previously learned; Teacher, bass lines.

C. Sight Reading and Listening.

D. Assignment.

1. Read Chapter 11, **The Melodic Soprano Voice.**

2. Play through the examples in Chapter 11.

Week 14

A. Theoretical. Discuss and answer questions pertinent to Chapter 11.

B. Application.

1. Play through the sample progressions I and II in Chapter 11.

2. Put a "G" Blues on the board with altered dominants. Class comps while individuals improvise using patterns or their own ideas.

3. Discuss with the individuals who played solos how their improvisation could be improved, e.g. remark on (a) phrasing, (b) time, (c) use of space, etc.

C. Sight Reading and Listening.

D. Assignment.

1. Have students analyze and write out voicings using alterations to any tune of their choice.

2. Read Chapter 12, **Sample Progessions for Further Study.**

Week 15

A. Theoretical. Discuss and answer questions pertinent to Chapter 12.

B. Application.

1. Play sample progressions offered in Chapter 12.

2. Painstakingly proceed through the bar by bar analysis of each sample realization to **Pennies From Heaven** and **The Lady Is A Tramp.**

3. Allow time for individual practice of last week's assignment, comping to the tune of choice.

C. Sight Reading and Listening.

D. Assignment.

1. Review

2. Practice tune of choice.

Week 16

A. Theoretical.

Review:

      1. Generic Voicings
      2. Miracle Voicings
      3. Polychord Fractions
      4. Diminished Voicings
      5. Half Step Preparation
      6. Tritone Substitutions
      7. Melodic Comping
      8. Sample Progressions

B. Application.

1. Allow time for individual practice of "tune of choice."

D. Assignment.

1. Study and

2. Practice

Week 17

Examination and individual performance of "tune of choice."

WHAT TWENTY-FIVE PROMINENT PROFESSIONAL MUSICIANS AND JAZZ EDUCATORS HAVE TO SAY ABOUT "VOICINGS":

"**Voicings** is a well organized treatment of common harmonic situations found in contemporary jazz. Anyone desiring to achieve a better understanding of this idiom will be well served by this book."

John LaPorta, Faculty, Berklee College, Boston

"**Voicings** is a brilliant, innovative and well-conceived book. The approach is original and educationally sound. **Voicings** should prove invaluable to teacher, performer, and student alike. It is a marvelous addition to jazz piano literature. I recommend it very highly."

David Baker, Faculty, Indiana University

"Mantooth's logical, sequential approach to piano voicings and comprehensive analyses of functional jazz harmonies should silence forever the cry of those in academia who view jazz as a bastard. His 'polychord fraction' concept is a rational synthesis of jazz and traditional theory which bespeaks his joint heritage in classical music and 'in the trenches' jazz. Tomorrow's jazz pianists will be in debt to Mr. Mantooth."

Dr. Metche Alexander, Freelance educator, Los Angeles area

"I recommend **Voicings** as a useful tool in the pursuit of a solid background in jazz harmony. The book contains a lot of useful information for both student and teacher."

Willie Pickens, Faculty, American Conservatory of Music, Chicago

---

"A real in-depth examination of what makes good piano players sound great. For the first time, an outstanding jazz pianist shares with us some of the secrets. An excellent book for the beginning and advanced jazz or classical pianist. A must for all music educators."

Gene Aitken, Director of Jazz Studies, University of Northern Colorado

---

"As a rhythm section clinician, I know this book will fill a void. Frank's 'down to earth' approach is easy to understand. I would recommend this book to both players and teachers. I know I'll use it."

Steve Houghton, Yamaha Drum Clinician Instructor, Percussion Institute, Hollywood

---

"This book is a thorough, well-organized presentation of precisely the material that I, as a woodwind player, need to teach jazz improvisation to pianists and to work with jazz ensemble and combo pianists. The listening list and course syllabus are valuable inclusions."

Laurie Marino, Faculty, Concordia College and Columbia College, Chicago

---

"I found this text to be very logical in the way it is laid out and thorough in its use of musical examples. I would certainly recommend it highly for anyone wishing to study harmonic relationships, whether they be pianists, arrangers, or composers."

Tom Bruner, L.A. based author and television musical director

"...long overdue...Finally, a text and study method available to help students develop choice, 'tasty', and appropriate jazz chord voicings. Frank has written a "gem" of a book that **really works!**"

Michael J. Irish

Mike Irish, Director of Jazz Studies,
University of Wisconsin/Stevens Point

"...enjoyable to read. Good examples and explanations...Great book! This fills an important gap in jazz piano materials...the current fourthy polychordal approach.

Dan Haerle

Dan Haerle, Faculty,
North Texas State University

"Finally someone has had both the insight and knowledge to fill in one of the weakest areas in our jazz education system...chord voicings for pianists. Not being a piano player myself, I have suffered through some extremely frustrating moments with young pianists trying to figure out what to play when they see "slashes" on the part instead of voicings. This will be one of our most valuable teaching tools and I know we'll all experience a sigh of relief. Thank you, Frank.

Bobby Shew

Bobby Shew

"This book is more than a much-needed system of generating good-sounding piano voicings. Frank divulges his best musical secrets in a comprehensive method. He covers what sounds good, why it does, and how to use it. It's a complete book for serious musicians at any level.

Kelly L. Sill

Kelly Sill, Freelance bassist and teacher, Chicago

"Frank Mantooth has written a super method to help pianists of all levels develop great sounding harmonies...am glad that you included a semesters' syllabus.

Craig Whittaker

Craig Whittaker, Director of Jazz Ensembles,
University of North Carolina at Greensboro

"**Voicings** is an original book by Frank Mantooth. It spells out the important basic fundamentals every pianist/writer should know. Every musician can benefit from this wonderful text. Duke Ellington once said, 'The secret is in the **voicings.**' The years of studying and experience are evident in this wonderful manuscript. I recommend it 100%...

Louie Bellson

Louie Bellson

"Dozens, maybe hundreds of stage band directors have asked how they should approach their 'pianist problems', and I've never had a neat, concise answer. Now I have...I'll start by telling them about this book."

Tom Banks

Tom Banks, Pianist, Educator,
C.B.S. Television personality, Edmonton

"This well reasoned, no-nonsense approach will go far in helping to solve piano voicing problems for all who seek this kind of information no matter their age or experience level...the ordinary player can improve immediately and the gifted player will find new doors to open..."

Floyd Standifer Jr.

Floyd Standifer Jr., Jazz trumpeter,
Teacher, Clinician, Seattle.

"**Voicings** is it . . . for those of us who have needed a straight forward, practical, and usable text to help solve voice leading problems, Frank Mantooth has given it to us. He has taken the mystery and fakery out of the jazz voicings to allow even the most traditionally oriented musician full understanding of his proven and practiced principles. A great resource for every performer, writer/arranger, and teacher."

Maj. James M. Bankhead, Commander/Conductor
U.S. Air Force Band, Washington, D.C.

"Thanks for thinking of me for an endorsement for **Voicings.** It's just what I would like to have to get some comping chops together myself . . . . . ."

Art Farmer

". . . this book offers practical applications of voicing concepts by giving musical examples for study and practice rather than suggestions for voicings in isolated contexts. In addition, this book presents step-by-step systems for voicing chords in the traditional jazz style. I think its a 'hit'."

John Radd, Faculty, University of Wisconsin

"For years, jazz keyboard greats have achieved an almost effortless, sophisticated sound through efficient chord voicings and economy of hand movement. In this book, Frank Mantooth effectively communicates how it's done. A valuable tool for any keyboard player.

Jeff Jarvis

". . . marvelous book! A truly original, comprehensive, economical and above all, practical approach to sophistication in chord voicings."

Bunky Green, Faculty, Chicago State University

"This book is extremely helpful in understanding about harmony and gives you a broader view on polychords. I recommend it to anyone who wants to improve their chord voicings."

Jack Petersen, Faculty,
North Texas State University

"Frank's knowledge and experience, combined with his down to earth approach have given us a text that will be indispensable to students, educators, and professionals.

Doug Beach, Publisher, Faculty,
Elmhurst College

"Even if I had never heard Tommy Flanagan, Herbie Hancock, or Hank Jones play a solo, they would be three of my favorite piano players. It's a pleasure to see a well-organized book that tells a piano player about a lot more than how to **solo** over a set of chord changes."

Howie Smith, Yamaha Saxophone Clinician,
Faculty, Cleveland State University

"Frank's book gives much needed information on newer sounding voicings and easy ways to achieve them. Everything he says is clear, direct, and usable. This book should be a part of each teacher's library. It fills in gaps and does it in a logical manner."

Jamey Aebersold